AS THE PROP TURNS

AS THE PROP TURNS

THE SOUL OF AN OLD AIRPLANE

BY JOHN WOOD

To Paddy, Clara, Maddie, and Tommy

The dangers of life are infinite, and among them is safety.

—Goethe

CONTENTS

—◆◆◆—

INTRODUCTION

—∭—

THIS IS THE STORY OF A WACO UPF-7, an antique open-cockpit airplane, still in the air nearly eighty years after delivery. It has trained military pilots, spread chemicals on crops, and, in later years, earned admiration as an aviation classic. It has been wrecked and rebuilt, from basket case to showpiece, several times, each revival requiring several thousand hours of labor.

This book isn't really about the airplane; inanimate objects don't have much of a story to tell. It is about the people who have flown it. They have many stories.

Some readers silently pronounce words as they read them. Let's start by sorting out different pronunciations, and their meanings, for the four-letter word W-A-C-O. In one case it is an acronym for the aircraft's builder, the Weaver Aircraft Company of Ohio. The *Wa* sounds like *water*—*Waco* rhymes with *taco*.

Waco is also a delightful city in central Texas, named after a Wichita Indian tribe, and in this meaning is pronounced "Way-ko." It was the site of a cruel tragedy in 1993, when David Koresh and the Branch Davidians were besieged there by the US government. Eighty people died as the compound burned, leading to the acronym *WACO*: We Ain't Comin' Out.

Finally, there is the word *wacko*, used to describe a crazy person. Consider this exercise: "There goes a wacko from Waco in his Waco." This would be pronounced, "There goes a 'whack-o' from 'Way-ko' in his 'Wha-ko.'" Got it?

THE EARLY DAYS

—m—

The newly-minted Waco entered service as an aerobatic trainer, just in time
to help bolster the ranks of pilots for the coming war!

WACO UPF-7, TAIL NUMBER NC29923,* WAS BORN OCTOBER 1, 1940, in Troy, Ohio. It has survived for eighty years; most airplanes don't get to be this old. It has served as a flying classroom, aerial jeep, agricultural implement, airport-day showpiece, and sunny-day joy machine.

The Waco was delivered into a world in crisis. Germany had invaded Poland a year earlier. Europe was at war, and the United States seemed certain to be pulled in. The Army Air Corps anticipated a massive scale-up of aerial conflict but was training only two hundred pilots per year. In 1939 there were only about seventy-four hundred commercial and private pilots between the ages of eighteen and thirty in the United States.

The Civilian Pilot Training Program (CPTP)[1] was created to address this need. Initially it had socioeconomic undertones as part of President Roosevelt's New Deal. It was intended to "air-condition" America's youth by training twenty thousand college students per year as pilots. The plan called for the government to pay colleges linked to flight schools for seventy-two hours of classroom training and thirty-five to fifty flight hours leading to the acquisition of a private pilot's license. The Army Air Corps was unenthusiastic about civilian training for military pilots, and the tension lasted for years.

The open-cockpit biplane was already obsolete as a primary trainer when the CPTP began. Obviously, instructors and students would find communication easier and more comfortable in an enclosed, heated cockpit. Much of the CPTP-sponsored initial instruction was conducted in the equivalent of a Piper Cub, which has an enclosed cockpit, better visibility, and more clearance between the wingtips and the ground.

So why did the Waco have an open cockpit? Some felt the pilot was better trained if his head was outside where he could experience the full range of sensations in flight—sights, sounds, vibrations, and variations in slipstream force accompanying changes in

---

* An aircraft's tail number is frequently used as its radio call sign. After initial contact, it is customary to shorten the call sign to the aircraft manufacturer and last three digits, as we will do henceforth: Waco '923.

airspeed. The Waco was typically used during the last ten hours of training to intro-duce the student to aerobatic flight, including loops, rolls, and spins.

One of the colleges selected for the CPTP was St. Martin's University in Lacey, Washington. It contracted with Buroker-Hicks Flying Service at the Olympia airport for flight training, and Waco '923 was delivered there in October 1940.

Gladys Buroker was a pioneering aviatrix of the Pacific Northwest. Her story is sum-marized on the Wall of Honor at the Smithsonian National Air and Space Museum:[2]

GLADYS WITH HER EXHIBITION PARACHUTE, 1935.

Gladys was born and raised north of Seattle, Washington. Her interest in aviation began as a child. At 18, a high school graduate, she made her first solo flight after only five hours of instruction. She flew an OX-5 Waco 10 on a September day in 1932. Her sense of adventure led her to parachute jumping with a barnstorming group, wing walking, and a motorcycle tour of the 48 states…

[In] 1937 Gladys married her longtime friend and flight instructor, Herb Buroker. In November she passed her written exam and flight test to receive her pilot's license. She passed her commercial flight test and flight instructor exams in 1938.

GLADYS' HUSBAND, HERB BUROKER DISMOUNTS FROM WACO '923.

After a ferry flight from the factory in Ohio, Waco '923 was put to work as an aerobatic trainer at the Olympia airport. In her memoir[3], Gladys writes of her early days at St. Martin's:

> When news got out about St. Martin's new flight program, 20 students immediately enrolled, and Father Gerald needed a ground school instructor—right away. I'm sure the college expected a man since St. Martin's was an all-male Catholic institution. Besides, women were supposed to be housewives. Imagine his surprise when he found through the grapevine that I was the only available certified ground school instructor in the Northwest.
>
> As I nervously left my car for the first day of classes I wondered what was in store for me. Pushing my way through a sea of men, I sensed them gawking, so I walked with my eyes straight ahead. "What is *she* doing here?" I could hear them whisper. I was, after all, the first woman to teach at St. Martin's. Even though I felt tense as a polecat, my first day in class went well, and within days my students had me scrambling to keep up with their excitement and curiosity. More than anything, they wanted to fly. If a woman taught the class, so be it. I became known among the students as "Assistant Father."

GLADYS WITH HER GROUND SCHOOL CLASS AND A FEMALE REPORTER, 1941.

One day Father Gerald walked into the classroom, his long black robe flowing behind his six-foot frame. He smiled broadly, as he always did, but I stiffened up at the podium for a moment, barely able to breathe. Before long I forgot he was there as I explained aerodynamics to my curious audience. As the students filed out, the Father stood up.

"I enjoyed your class tremendously," he said, adjusting the crucifix dangling from a heavy chain around his neck. "It would be such a pleasure to fly." I broke into a big grin, feeling like I'd just jumped over the moon.

The attack on Pearl Harbor on December 7, 1941, brought dramatic changes to the flight school. Kaiser Shipyards in Portland–Vancouver and Boeing Aircraft Company in Seattle were considered key targets as the United States prepared for a Japanese invasion of the Northwest. The Civil Aeronautics Board moved all civilian aviation well inland to clear the air for military protection of the coast. The Army Air Corps notified the Buroker-Hicks flight school that the Olympia airport would be taken over by a squadron of Lockheed P-38 fighters moved from McChord Field.

WACO '923 IS THE BACKDROP FOR THE FIRST ST. MARTIN'S CPTP SECONDARY CLASS IN OLYMPIA, WASHINGTON, 1941. NOTE PARACHUTES WORN DURING AEROBATIC FLIGHT.

The flight school relocated to Pasco in eastern Washington. It took a great effort to locate a hangar, study hall, and housing; St. Martin's provided busing to an extension campus. Alas, only four weeks after the flight school moved in, the navy decided the Pasco airport would be an excellent training location and took command of the site

Waco '923 and the flight school were on the move again, this time to Weeks Field in Coeur d'Alene, Idaho. This airfield had two turf runways, a small hangar, and no electricity, water, or telephone.[4] The flight school built a new hangar, and an abandoned camp building was hauled in for use as a flight office. The CAA opened another nearby airport as a backup in case of a Pacific-coast invasion.

Another change occurred after the Pearl Harbor attack—the training scheme tightened. Previous graduates of the Civilian Pilot Training Program had the option to apply as military pilots. After Pearl Harbor, the program was rebranded the War Training Service (WTS), and graduates were contractually bound to join the military. The flight school had already been notified that their CPTP contract would terminate when the last class of St. Martin's students graduated. The WTS issued a new contract, requiring changes to a military flight curriculum. Army and navy students poured in, stretching housing facilities in Coeur d'Alene, a town of twelve thousand residents.

WEEK'S FIELD, COEUR D'ALENE, IDAHO, 1943.

WEEK'S FIELD IS NOW COEUR D'ALENE'S FAIRGROUNDS, 2018.

In her memoir, Gladys writes of the challenges this new contract posed:

> That summer (1942) the WTS added night flying to the primary training program, a wrinkle we had not expected. Since most of our aircraft did not come equipped, Herb ran them through the shop to install navigation lights wired to a battery. For runway lights, we loaded a pickup bed with kerosene lanterns. A half hour before dusk, the driver slowly steered along the runway's edge, and a crewman would drop a lantern every thirty feet or so, lining both sides with what looked like a string of illuminated pearls from the air. The morning crew would follow the same route, retrieving the lanterns to trim wicks, clean globes and fill them with kerosene.
>
> The Navy, facing an emergency shortage of flight instructors, offered commissions to young men with 140 hours of civilian training who could meet Navy requirements. They would complete several months of school at Coeur d'Alene and then proceed as flight instructors to Navy training bases at New Orleans or Pensacola. Once underway, I found the Navy course the most relaxed teaching I'd ever done. The officers were experienced pilots, so we had a blast doing aerobatics in the Waco.
>
> "Expect forty-seven cross-country students," the commander of Fort George Wright in Spokane told us over the phone. They would begin arriving February 1943 with flight gear, parachutes and uniforms and would eventually turn our cross-country program into the largest west of the Mississippi. Most of the pilots we taught were older men from all walks of life who wanted to help with the war effort as instructors or ferry pilots.

The flight training was customized and multifaceted. The location in Coeur d'Alene meant students were exposed to the high winds of the prairie as well as mountain flying, both ideal for training cadets entering the Ferry Command, which flew supplies and men in and out of the war zone. By 1943 their program had grown to thirty-eight flight instructors and two hundred students. Gladys goes on to mention another challenge the program faced:

Although we felt confident all contingencies had been covered for night flying, we could never have predicted one hazard. The airport was unfenced. Pat O'Grady, our youngest instructor at twenty, was soloing a student one night in the spring of '43. A talented pilot and promising teacher, Pat was still wet behind the ears in many ways. When introduced I remember thinking, "This boy has a lot to learn." Although Pat looked all man with his flaming red hair and ruddy complexion, his high-water plaid pants and wide eyes told us about his maturity.

PATRICK O'GRADY IS ALL SMILES WITH WACO '923, COEUR D'ALENE, IDAHO, 1942.

Pat stood on the runway this particular evening, watching a student fly his solo pattern and make landings in a Piper J5. Lining up with the runway and dropping smoothly in for the third time, the student passed in and out of Pat's vision, nearly down and in perfect form. Then came a sickening crunch. Horrified, Pat dropped his clipboard and sprinted into the dark only to find the blood-spattered Piper upside down. Now out of his seat belt, the dazed student climbed onto the wing and staggered down its length, leaving tracks where he stepped through the fabric—crunch, crunch, crunch.

"Lay down," Pat shouted, helping the boy to the ground. Tearing off his shirt, Pat wiped blood from the student's face, arms, torso and legs, feeling for cuts and broken bones but not finding a scratch. After a quick survey of the area, Pat solved the mystery. A farmer must have left a gate open, his unlucky horse winning a one-way ticket to horsey heaven. The rest of us thought it hilarious that Pat of all people had the misfortune to be teaching that night. Pat had worked for us for a year by that time, had trained lots of cadets, and could fly like an ace. What he longed for was action.

INSTRUCTOR PAT WITH HIS FIRST CLASS IN COEUR D'ALENE, 1942. A FORMER STUDENT NOTED THAT DURING INVERTED FLIGHT, HE LIKED TO SING LOUDLY THROUGH THE GOSPORT SPEAKING TUBE THAT CONNECTED THEM.

In 1943 Pat accepted a direct commission in the army Air Transport Command, and in early 1945 he departed for the China-Burma-India theater, where he logged 754 combat hours flying seventy-nine round trips over "The Hump." On his return he remained in active reserve, flying P-51s and B-26s in Portland, Oregon. He finished his military career as brigadier general commanding the Oregon Air National Guard. In November 1946, immediately after the war, Pat helped develop West Coast Airlines, the precursor of Air West, Hughes Airwest, and Republic. Thirty-six years later, Captain Pat O'Grady would retire from Republic Airlines number one in seniority out of 1,875 pilots. He accumulated thirty-six thousand accident-free flight hours in 120 aircraft makes and models.[5]

COLONEL O'GRADY, THIRD FROM LEFT, LEADS THE OREGON AIR NATIONAL GUARD TEAM AT THE 1970 WILLIAM TELL AIR-TO-AIR WEAPONS MEET. NAMED FOR THE LEGENDARY SWISS CROSSBOWMAN WHO SHOT AN APPLE OFF HIS SON'S HEAD, THE WEEKLONG COMPETITION TESTED THE SKILLS OF PILOTS, WEAPONS LOAD TEAMS, MAINTENANCE TECHNICIANS, AND AIR WEAPONS CONTROLLERS.

On receiving a photograph of the Waco taken sixty-three years later, Pat writes this 2005 letter:

> My what a nice-looking bird. Better than when it came from the factory. The only difference was the prop and the color. In 1942 the wings were yellow, and the fuselage was blue and of course it had a metal prop. The minute you mentioned tail number NC29923 I recognized it immediately as I believe it is still printed on the cheeks of my rear from the three hundred hours, I instructed in it 1942–43. I enjoyed flying the bird as it was my first open cockpit and aerobatic experience.
>
> About the UPF-7; it was a sturdy trainer, almost impossible to hurt it in the air. The elevator movement was rather long which made it sometimes hard for the student to get enough forward elevator to keep the nose up while doing rolls or prolonged inverted flight. I solved this by having the student reach forward and hold one of the fuselage tubes for leverage. It worked for me too. Landings were easy except on asphalt. If you didn't keep it straight, it would be a wing down and drag an aileron. I had a solo student do that once, but that was the only mishap I had with the bird. The landing gear was wide, and not narrow like the Stearman. Stearmans tended to ground loop but the UPF-7 didn't. One thing I did demonstrate to the students before they graduated was inverted spins. I felt they should know how to get out of one if they got into one.
>
> Now about Coeur d'Alene, Idaho. Flying in an open cockpit airplane in the winter is <u>Cold,</u> especially at ten degrees below zero. However, the War was on and we had class dates to complete, so we pressed on. I was so cold sometimes that I couldn't get out of the front cockpit during refueling because if I did, I wouldn't be able to get back in. I will say this, we were young and just think, we were getting paid for flying. I really think we would have done it for nothing.

Meanwhile, the military had scaled up its own cadet-training activity and moved pilots into heavier, faster, more complex aircraft that were not in civilian hands. The army and navy always felt that pure military training screened out those who could not make the cut and produced a better military pilot. The civilian program was no longer needed even though it had taught over four hundred thousand pilots to fly, including hundreds of women and African Americans.

One Sunday morning in January 1944, Buroker-Hicks Flying Service received a telegram from the WTS stating all training activities would end that day. In less than twenty-four hours, the business would return to commercial activities as governed by wartime regulations. Waco '923 was out of a job and was sold back to the US government for $6,618 in May of that year.

PATRICK O'GRADY'S OUTFIT FOR OPEN COCKPIT WINTER FLYING IN IDAHO, 1942.

After the war, Herb and Gladys received a contract from the Veterans Administration for flight training. Wall of Honor at the Smithsonian National Air and Space Museum concludes:

A hangar fire in 1950 prompted a change of life for the couple. In the late 1960s Gladys embarked on a second career as a licensed practical nurse. She remained actively involved with aviation and participated in the development of the Henley Aerodrome at Athol, Idaho, a base for vintage airplanes. She flew a hot air balloon on the opening day at the Expo '74 World's Fair in Spokane, Washington.

In retirement she became manager of flight operations for the new owner of the aerodrome. She flew gliders and, on occasion, the Pawnee tow plane and the Cessna 182 "jump" plane. At the end of the season in 1990 she chose to retire. Gladys Buroker represents that indomitable will that sparks all who fly.

GLADYS BUROKER FLYING WACO UPF-7 NC29926 FOR AN ADVERTISING BANNER PICKUP, 1947. A HOOK, NOT VISIBLE BEHIND THE AIRCRAFT, IS ABOUT TO CATCH THE ROPE STRUNG BETWEEN TWO POLES.

GLADYS STRAPPING A FRIEND IN FOR A GLIDER RIDE AT AGE SEVENTY-FOUR, 1988.

FREIGHT DOG AND THE MOUNTAIN

—⁓—

Waco '923 gave a number of pilots their first taste of aerobatics. Rudolph Libra survived many missions in the South Pacific, only to be killed in a 1958 air cargo crash.

RUDOLF LIBRA'S LIFE INTERSECTED WITH WACO '923 IN Coeur d'Alene, Idaho. Rudy was born in Minnesota in 1917 and grew up during the Great Depression. To offset these difficult times, FDR created the Civilian Conservation Corps (CCC), and Rudy enlisted. MNopedia, a website that chronicles Minnesota history, describes the program's effects.[1] This New Deal program offered meaningful work to young men with few employment prospects. It resulted in a lasting legacy of forestry, soil, and water conservation, as well as enhancements to Minnesota's state and national parks...

RUDY (RIGHT) WITH TEENAGE FRIENDS, 1933.

To qualify, candidates had to be healthy U.S. citizens, out of school, unemployed, unmarried, and on public assistance. Recruits reported to an assigned camp for a period of six months. Those with a good work record had the option to sign up for a second six-month term. Each man received thirty dollars per month. Enrollees were required to send twenty-five dollars home to their families, and kept five dollars for personal use...

Minnesota CCC projects centered mainly on forestry and state and national park projects. They also supported soil and water conservation. The men in forest camps cut and cleared brush to help conserve existing forests and planted 123,607,000 trees.

RUDY MOVING SUPPLIES TO A REMOTE CIVILIAN CONSERVATION CORPS (CCC) CAMP NEAR WANLESS, MINNESOTA.

The CCC program peaked in Minnesota in 1935 with 104 active camps. Enrollment began to decline in the early 1940s as young men joined the military for World War II and as the economy began to rebound. All of Minnesota's camps closed in 1942. More than seventy-seven thousand Minnesota men found employment with the program.

RUDY LEARNED THAT NONCOLLEGE PRELIMINARY FLIGHT TRAINING SCHOLARSHIPS WERE BEING OFFERED BY THE CIVIL AVIATION AUTHORITY IN OREGON. HE WAS ACCEPTED AT THE OREGON INSTITUTE OF TECHNOLOGY, MOVED TO PORTLAND, AND TRAINED AT THE SWAN ISLAND AIRPORT, LATER CONVERTED TO A SHIPYARD.

RUDY SITS ON A WACO WING IN PORTLAND WITH AN APPREHENSIVE
STUDENT'S LOOK AND THE HANDS OF A CONCERT PIANIST.

RUDY, RIGHT, WITH WACO '923 IN COEUR D'ALENE, IDAHO, MAY 1942,
AFTER CIVILIAN TRAINING WAS MOVED AWAY FROM THE PACIFIC COAST. THE
AUTHOR'S DISCOVERY OF THIS PHOTO PUT THE BOOK IN MOTION.

RUDY, SECOND LEFT, JOINED THE ARMY AIR CORPS AND QUALIFIED IN THE DOUGLAS
C-47 AT THE ARMY AIR FIELD IN PALM SPRINGS, CALIFORNIA. HE WAS ASSIGNED TO THE
SOUTHWEST PACIFIC WING OF THE PACIFIC DIVISION OF THE AIR TRANSPORT COMMAND.
THIS GROUP WAS TASKED WITH MOVING TROOPS AND MATERIAL FROM AUSTRALIA TO NEW
GUINEA AS GENERAL DOUGLAS MACARTHUR MOVED INEXORABLY TOWARD JAPAN.

Rudy was one of many young men who left the CCC to join the war effort overseas. Staff Sergeant Jack Seese, radio operator, recalls the long trip they embarked on across the vast ocean. From Michigan, the crews flew to California, where they joined a group of C-47s headed for the South Pacific. In June 1944 they departed from Hamilton Field to Hickam Field, Honolulu, on a C-47 that had been equipped with an auxiliary gas tank in the cargo hold for the fifteen-hour trip. From Honolulu the aircraft proceeded to Christmas Island, Canton Island, Fiji, New Caledonia., then on to their destination, Ipswich, Australia. The flight time totaled fifty-four hours over eight days.

Jack writes in his memoir:[2]

> One of the happenings that we had was losing an engine along the north coast of New Guinea between Finschhafen and Hollandia. We couldn't maintain altitude since we had one engine feathered, and we were slowly descending to 500 feet. During this time the co-pilot went to the cargo hold and eventually came back past the radio space with his flight suit wringing wet and told me he had jettisoned all our cargo. The cargo happened to be boxes of Atabrine tablets which were used to delay malaria until we returned to the U.S.A. I looked into the cargo area and it was empty. At this time, we were off the coast of New Guinea opposite Wewak, which was one of the areas General McArthur leapfrogged to let the Japanese "wither on the vine". We then held our altitude and made an emergency landing at Atiape, which was an airfield the Australians held. We stayed overnight and had our plane repaired and proceeded on to Hollandia.

Rather than waste resources on conquering every Japanese stronghold, General MacArthur decided to hop over some and cut the Japanese supply line from the motherland. US pilots were wary of the Wewak area because there were thought to be twenty thousand starving Japanese soldiers in the jungle who would not be courteous to a downed aircrewman.

Rudy's copilot was Herb Hart,[3] who began training under the CPTP at San Mateo Junior College. He completed primary flight training at San Francisco International Airport. Herb was transferred to Frederick Field in Oklahoma for advanced twin-engine training and graduated with Class 44B. His checkout in the C-47 consisted of riding in the back with other cadets, each taking turns at a few takeoffs and landings.

PILOT RUDY LIBRA, COPILOT HERBERT HART, AND RADIOMAN WILLIAM
MEYERS ON THEIR C-47 WING IN NEW GUINEA.

Herb rode as a passenger to Australia, where he was paired with another pilot and told to fly twenty-one civilians to New Guinea. Herb had made only two landings in a C-47, and neither man had more than two flight hours in the aircraft. Herb asked his copilot, "Do you know how to start this thing?" They got it running, and Herb's landing in New Guinea turned into three landings as they bounced down the runway. On their return trip, Herb could tell from passenger's faces they were thinking: "Oh my God, these same two are going to fly us back?"

Back at the base, both pilots were reassigned as copilots, Herb* with Rudy Libra. They were based first in Townsville, Australia, and then Finschhafen, New Guinea. In later correspondence, Herb remembers this time fondly:

> I flew many hours with Rudy. It was the greatest period of my time in the service. More than once we stayed up late at the club. Next morning, after an early takeoff, one of us would keep an eye on the autopilot while the other one napped. I remember one time we both drifted off to sleep. I awoke to see the mountains near Port Moresby in front of us and only minutes away. Luck was with us and we learned a lesson.

RUDY TAKES A BREAK IN FINSCHHAFEN, NEW GUINEA.

---

* Herb Hart later made first pilot. After the war he spent his career as an educator, teaching high school art class in the San Francisco area. At age ninety-seven, he has vivid memories of his time in the service.

We used the autopilot to play jokes a few times. One of us would
get out of our seat, and wander back into the cabin, playing host
pilot and chatting with passengers. After a while the other pilot,
with the C-47 on autopilot, would get, up leaving the front office
vacant. Then a passenger would be invited to go up front and see
what the cockpit was like. You can imagine the result, seeing the
empty pilot seats with only the radio operator on the job.

HERB HART (CENTER) WITH A FELLOW AIRMAN ON BONDI BEACH, SYDNEY, AUSTRALIA, ON LEAVE FROM
NEW GUINEA IN 1945. AUSSIE GIS WERE SHIPPED OVERSEAS TO FIGHT. AMERICAN SOLDIERS WERE IN
DEMAND. THOUSANDS OF AUSTRALIAN WOMEN MARRIED AMERICAN SERVICEMEN BASED DOWN UNDER, AND
LATER MOVED TO THE UNITED STATES. HERB DID NOT BRING HOME A WAR BRIDE; HE MARRIED LATER.

Rudy had another favorite prank. When transporting troops, he would bring aboard
a bag of empty beer cans and hide it in the cockpit. After takeoff, he and his copilot
would periodically roll a can back down the aisle into the cabin, creating worry among
passengers that their crew was drinking on the job.

In yet another stunt, after passengers were loaded, the pilot would climb in the rear door and, instead of heading to the cockpit, would sit on the chemical toilet in the tail and stare ahead with a blank expression. The copilot would leave the cockpit and head back through the cabin, saying loudly, "Lieutenant, you are flying us this morning; get up here." With that the pilot would slowly make his way forward to the copilot's seat. Again, the copilot would make a scene, telling the pilot, "No, no, you're in the left seat." All this to bolster passengers' confidence.

THE UNITED STATES ARMY

presents

IRVING BERLIN'S
ALL-SOLDIER-SHOW

"THIS IS THE ARMY"

Music and Lyrics by Irving Berlin.
Musical Numbers and Dances Staged by Sgt. Robert Sidney.
Scenery Designed by Lt. John Koenig.
Costumes Designed by Sgt. Joseph Fretwell, III.
Musical Director, Sgt. Milton Rosenstock.
Entire Production Staged under the Personal Direction of Mr. Berlin.
Production in the Southwest Pacific Area under Supervision of United States Army SWPA Special Services Section.

OVERTURE .. .. This Is the Army Orchestra
Captain: Cpl. Ralph Magelssen; Sgt. of the Guard: Sgt. Alan Manson; Guards: Cpl. John Draper and Pvt. Hampton Thomas.
OPENING CHORUS .. .. The Company
"THIS IS THE ARMY, Mr. JONES."
Sung by The Selectees: Sgt. Julie Oshins, Cpl. William Roerich, Cpl. Hank Henry, Pfc. Henry Jones, Pfc. Arthur Gilmour, Pvt. John Hederman and Pvt. Daniel Longo.
SGT. DICK BERNIE.
"I'M GETTING TIRED SO I CAN SLEEP"

A TISSUE-THIN PROGRAM RECORDED RUDY'S ATTENDANCE IN NEW GUINEA OF *THIS IS THE ARMY*, A POPULAR MORALE-BOOSTING SHOW THAT TOURED MILITARY BASES DURING WORLD WAR II.

Herb's account continues: My tentmate heard of an exciting discovery and decided to take his C-47 on a sightseeing tour. With a little difficulty he found the settlement in a remote valley and proceeded to drop down to get a good look by buzzing the natives. With gear extended and full flaps he dragged the populated area. On the second pass he was attacked by a warrior who tried to down the big bird with a spear that flew harmlessly over the wing. Still gawking at the fascinating sights, the pilot suddenly became aware that he was at the end of a valley with a big mountain in front of him. He shoved propeller pitch levers forward, applied full throttle, pulled up the gear and flaps and staggered over the last ridge.

This same pilot and his copilot missed a big item on the takeoff checklist, forgetting to lock the tailwheel, as they swung on to the runway for a rolling takeoff. He was still trying to get control of the C-47 as the plane roared along just shy of takeoff speed, but it went off the side of the runway. The plane was loaded with gas and caught fire, but not before the crew escaped with only a few scratches. He had no idea how valuable the cargo was until he learned it included discharge papers for a soldier who had served a long time in New Guinea.

AIRCRAFT THAT WERE WRECKED ON LANDING IN NEW GUINEA WERE BULLDOZED OFF THE RUNWAY. SCAVENGING THE REMAINS WAS A FAVORITE PASTIME FOR RUDY AND HERB.

Herb Hart has retained, in his scrapbook, an October 1945 magazine article announcing the end of the Southwest Pacific Wing, in which he served:

After fourteen months, the Southwest Pacific Wing of the Pacific Division of the widespread Air Transport Command has ceased operation.

What makes this important is that the Southwest Wing established just about the highest single record of military air transport operations in the world. It flew something like 47,000,000 miles in fourteen months in twin-engine Douglas C-47 cargo planes over jungle and water in none-to-favorable weather conditions, and never so much as lost a pound of freight or scratched a single passenger. And virtually every flight crew in the Wing was composed of lads from nineteen to twenty-five years of age, right out of training schools and without a single bit of prior aviation experience.

Old-timers have watched the Wing with amazement. There were no airways, no radio aids, poor airfields, meager weather information, and no airline supervision at the top—yet the boys ended up with a 100 percent safety record.

The routes extended from Australia over New Guinea (high mountains and much of the time abominable weather) and on up through the entire Philippine archipelago. Overwater routes were as much as 1,000 miles in twin-engine airplanes.

Experts give credit first of all to thorough Army training and secondly to the reliable and sturdy C-47 which has established records all over the world. But most of the pilots started right in flying these transports with only 300 to 400 hours. A commercial airline would shudder at the thought.

After their discharge, Rudy and Herb moved to Stockton, California. In July 1946 they traveled to a military aircraft boneyard in Arizona and paid $450 for a surplus Vultee BT-13A aircraft, affectionately known as the "Vultee Vibrator." This aircraft was the next step up in basic training for many World War II cadets. It was heavier, with a

450-horsepower engine, controllable-pitch propeller, and flaps. With the canopies slid back, the plane was ideal for weekend flying with friends and family.

RUDY AND WIFE, ANNA MARIA, IN THEIR SURPLUS VULTEE BT-13A OVER THE CALIFORNIA DESERT.

In the late 1940s, Rudy moved to Southern California, and the partners decided to sell the aircraft to a crop duster, who wanted the engine for his Stearman biplane. This doubled its horsepower and allowed the Stearman to carry more dust or liquid. Their Vultee was struck from the FAA registry in 1977.

Rudy wrote a magazine article in 1950 describing his misadventures as a civilian pilot:[4]

> "We lost again?" I asked the copilot sadly.
>
> "Yeh...don't know where the 'ell we are—exactly, that is. Read me the road map again," he answered with a half-grin. Give two ex-Berlin Airlift pilots a new Navion to deliver across the country

and life suddenly becomes complicated. We'd both been flying long enough to know better: 5,000-odd hours each in the last 12 or 14 years. But it had been about eight years since either of us had flown anything smaller than a DC-3.

"Shucks, this'll be a cinch vacation trip," I had told Stan Mitchem when we set up this delivery flight from the Ryan factory in San Diego to Reading, Pennsylvania. I should have kept my big mouth shut.

Just how wrong can a guy be? If we hadn't brought along that road map for the return trip via Studebaker, we'd have never made it. I'd completely forgotten that compared to these little airplanes—no autopilot, no radio operator's compartment for navigation, no crew chief, and no "powder room"—flying a C-54 is a lazy-man's way of going places. But it was interesting to say the least.

At daylight the next morning it was drizzly with a solid overcast at 1,500 feet. That's no trouble in a C-54—you just file an instrument clearance and plow up on top. But Lloyd's of London ferry insurance doesn't cover night or instrument flight in a single-engine airplane. So four sleepy people sat around in the San Diego Weather Bureau and bothered the man juggling the isobars.

The trip took three long days with predictable adventures.

While flying in the South West Pacific, Rudy made friends with other pilots who would be valuable contacts in his civilian career. In December 1950, Rudy became a "freight dog," an affectionate term for pilots who fly packages in old airplanes while most everyone else is sleeping. Rudy joined Flying Tiger Line[5] as employee number 4877, initially flying the Curtiss-Wright C-46.

FIRST OFFICER RUDY LIBRA BOARDS A CURTISS WRIGHT C-46
AIRCRAFT OPERATED BY FLYING TIGER LINE.

The Flying Tiger air freight line was founded in 1946 by returning veterans who sensed a market along the west coast of the United States and Mexico. Initially flying military surplus piston aircraft, Flying Tiger acquired jet air freighters, participated in the Korean and Vietnam airlifts, and in 1979 surpassed Pan Am to become the world's largest air cargo carrier. In 1978, the US dropped government regulation[6] of airline routes and prices. Flying Tiger struggled with losses after deregulation[7] and was sold to Federal Express in 1988.

FROM 1957 UNTIL 1962, LOCKHEED SUPER CONSTELLATIONS WERE
THE BACKBONE OF FLYING TIGER'S OPERATIONS.

Rudy's last flight on this earth was on September 9, 1958; he was in the right seat of a Lockheed L-1049H Super Constellation flying from California to Japan.[7] The last leg was over seventeen hundred nautical miles from Wake Island to Tachikawa Air Base outside Tokyo. The nearly new Flying Tiger Line aircraft was carrying fifteen and a half tons of military cargo. While approaching Tachikawa AFB in poor weather conditions, the four-engine aircraft struck the slope of Mount Ōyama (forty-one hundred feet high), located fifteen miles southwest of the air base.

RUDY LIBRA, FROM HIS CALIFORNIA NEWSPAPER OBITUARY.

The aircraft disintegrated on impact, killing all on board—two pilots, flight engineer, navigator, two flight attendants, and two military couriers.[8] The mountain range had already taken other victims bound for the same airport in instrument flight conditions. In 1950, a US Air Force C-54 transport flying from the Philippines to Tachikawa descended prematurely and collided with Mount Hiru, killing all thirty-five people on board.[9]

Rudy's aircraft was being radar vectored westbound to intercept the northbound final approach course to Tachikawa. The signal to turn right would have been the swing of a localizer needle on a horizontal situation indicator. Each pilot had one of these gauges, but for some reason, they missed the turn and flew through the extended runway centerline straight into the mountain. A subsequent investigation by Flying Tiger Lines offered the possibility that a critical inverter power supply had failed and the instruments did not display properly. Other Super Constellations were modified such that a loud buzzer would sound with this failure.

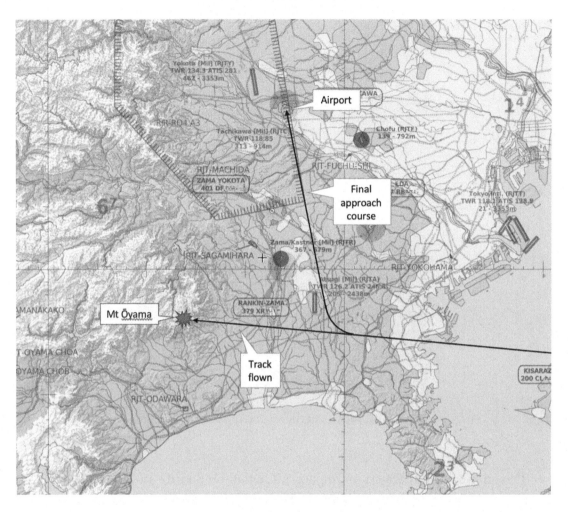

DURING DESCENT IN TOKYO AIRSPACE, THE AIRCRAFT WAS SUPPOSED TO TURN NORTH ON FINAL APPROACH TO THE AIRPORT. INSTEAD IT CONTINUED WEST INTO THE MOUNTAIN.

The airline raised funds to assist ten children left by the crew.[10] The accident occurred on the first birthday of Rudy's son Gary. He reports that the president of Flying Tiger Lines later visited his mother and said that the ground controller at the air base was handling two aircraft on arrival and may have gotten them confused. An alert radar operator would have noticed that the aircraft missed the turn and alerted the crew.[11]

RUDY LIBRA DIED ON HIS SON GARY'S FIRST BIRTHDAY, AND HIS WIFE,
ANNA MARIA, WAS PREGNANT WITH GARY'S BROTHER.

IN 1983, ANNA MARIA MARRIED VASEK POLAK, A WELL KNOWN CAR
DEALER AND RACE CAR DRIVER. SHE DIED IN 1993.

The type of accident that killed Rudy is now known as CFIT—Controlled Flight Into Terrain—wherein a perfectly good aircraft is inadvertently flown into the ground. Many times, the aircraft almost makes it over the top, which was the case with the Super Constellation. The wreckage was scattered over two miles. Terrain avoidance by aircraft was quite primitive in 1958. This was a long, overwater flight with no landmarks or radio beacons, so position was determined by celestial navigation—a sextant, a watch, computation tables, and a map. Near the Japanese coast, the crew would have used low-frequency and VHF radio aids to head to the airport, followed by radar vectors from a ground controller.

The challenge was maintaining "situational awareness," keeping a three-dimensional map in your head updated even as rain beat on the windscreen and the aircraft was buffeted by turbulence. Losing this awareness meant that one minute you were flying a nearly new, 120,000-pound, 4-engine, 13,000-horsepower, 300-mile-per-hour machine, and the next second you were dead.

The most notorious CFIT accident was Air New Zealand Flight 901, which crashed on a sightseeing flight over Antarctica in 1979, killing 257 people. The crew was unaware of changes to their flight plan and collided with Mount Erebus. According to Boeing, "Since the beginning of commercial jet operations, more than 9,000 deaths have resulted because of airplanes inadvertently flying into terrain, water or an obstacle."

Thanks to GPS, the Space Shuttle, and modern avionics, today's aircraft carry an enhanced terrain-avoidance system that has averted many disasters. The GPS receiver means aircraft position is constantly known. A specialized radar in the Space Shuttle was used to map the earth's topography. Other obstacles such as television towers and power lines are added to the computerized map. A pilot flying too close to an obstacle, say at night or in the clouds, receives an audible warning of "terrain, terrain" or "pull up, pull up!" The areas around airports receive special treatment to avoid false alarms on takeoff and landing.

DEATH AND TAXES

—⁓—

Another wartime pilot, Stanley Trohimovich, cut his teeth in Waco '923 before serving with distinction in the Pacific. Later he gained dubious notoriety through his Quixotic campaign as a tax protestor.

STANLEY TROHIMOVICH GREW UP AROUND CARS. HIS FAMILY ran a small business in Elma, Washington: two gas pumps, groceries, auto parts, and repair. He was a good student, more interested in academics than athletics. The war started the year after Stan graduated from high school. Buroker-Hicks Flying Service recruited student pilots at St. Martin's University, and he signed up. If Stan was going to serve in the military, he wanted to be a pilot.

STAN TROHIMOVICH (BACK ROW, THIRD FROM RIGHT) WITH HIS CPTP CLASS AT
ST. MARTIN'S COLLEGE IN 1942. WACO '923 IS IN THE BACKGROUND.

He spent spring break in 1942 flying at Coeur d'Alene, flying Waco '923, and earned his private pilot's license that summer. Stan took the Army Air Corps physical exam, passed, and waited to hear from Uncle Sam. The letter came in February 1943, and he subsequently began cadet flight training in Arizona and California. Then a roadblock went up: Stan failed an eye examination. His eyes would not converge when looking at the same spot. He went home to an optometrist, who prescribed eye exercises with a machine. Stan retook and passed the test.

LIEUTENANT STANLEY TROHIMOVICH WITH HIS PILOT'S WINGS.

Back in training, Stan moved to twin-engine aircraft. He flew the Cessna AT-17 Bobcat. Better known as the "Bamboo Bomber," it was cut from the same cloth as the Waco—made mostly of wood, welded tubing, and fabric. The Air Corps recognized Stan's flying and people skills and made him a flight instructor. He instructed students in the Curtiss-Wright AT-9[9] Jeep, a twin-engine airplane with such nasty flying characteristics that it was not released to civilians after the war.

TRAUB, JEAN R.
TRIMBLE, JACK D.
TROHIMOVICH, STANLEY J.
TRUDEAU, PAUL R.
TRYON, BEN L.

TULLEY, JAMES G.
UPSHER, SIDNEY P.
VAN METER, CLARENCE M.
VERUTTI, VALANCE C.
WALTER, ALBERT C.

STAN ADVANCED TO TWIN-ENGINE CADET TRAINING IN DOUGLAS, ARIZONA.

By 1944 Stan was flying the North American B-25 medium bomber,[2] an aircraft made famous by Jimmy Doolittle in his daring raid of Tokyo from the aircraft carrier *Hornet* at the beginning of the war. Stan joined the 345th Bombardment Group, the "Air Apaches," in Greenville, South Carolina. They were equipped with the B-25J, the last of the series. It was a deadly flying gunship, carrying eighteen fifty-caliber machine guns. No other main-series production bomber of World War II carried as many guns. The plane was designed as a strafing platform for the Pacific theater, a weapon operating at treetop level against land targets and at wavetop against shipping.

Stan served as a flight instructor in an advanced twin-engine school and was left behind, as most of his class shipped out to Asia-Pacific with the Air Apaches. The 345th's casualty rate was high in 1944, and Stan lost his two closest friends. He came to believe he had literally dodged a bullet. Strafing and bombing the Japanese just above the ground or water was dangerous business. Many airplanes returned with bullet holes.

B-25s bombing and strafing Japanese vessels, 1945.

Because the attacks were flown so low, there was little chance of using a parachute to escape a crippled aircraft. The alternative was ditching in the ocean with the very real possibility of being captured by the Japanese. Some airmen were so frightened by this prospect they vowed to shoot themselves with their service pistols rather than meet this fate.

Jay Stout, in his book *Air Apaches*, recounts the murder of a B-25 crew:

> They were typical of the sorts of atrocities committed by the monster state that was the Empire of Japan. During the period leading up to World War II and during the war itself, the Japanese brutalized virtually every population over whom they held sway, often slaughtering civilians on an industrial scale. The most infamous example was the "Rape of Nanking," during which an estimated three hundred thousand Chinese civilians—including women and children—were viciously slain, often with bayonets or swords. And throughout Asia, millions more were pitilessly butchered, worked to death, or starved...
>
> That Japan abused its prisoners of war is well documented and undisputed outside Japan. Aside from beatings, tortures, and starvation, murder was commonplace...The Japanese also cannibalized prisoners, sometimes cutting flesh from them while they were still alive. In fact, one Japanese unit codified the practice when it issued an instructional memorandum titled "Order Regarding Eating the Flesh of American Flyers."

Beginning in March 1945, Stan flew twenty-five combat missions in the B-25J over China, Formosa, Korea, the Philippines, and Japan. He bombed and strafed sugar mills, radar stations, villages, and ships. A few days after the first atomic bomb fell on Hiroshima, he shared credit with another pilot in sinking a six-thousand-ton Japanese merchant ship, code-named "Sugar Baker Love," in the Korea Strait.

With the Japanese surrender on August 14, 1945, the United Stated broadcast instructions ordering the emperor to send government officials to Ie Shima to be transported to the surrender ceremony. They were to travel in unarmed "Betty" bombers painted white with large green crosses.

Jay Stout's account in *Air Apaches* continues:

> ...B-25s of the Air Apaches were selected to escort the aircraft carrying the Japanese representatives to Ie Shima. The 345th's men recognized it as the great honor it was—a tribute to the hurt they had done the enemy and to the sacrifices they had endured.

345th Escorts Japanese Emissaries to IE-Shima

19 AUG. 1945

MAJOR McCLURE PICKS
UP JAP PLANES BELOW
KYUSHU

OVER STRIP, FLANKED
BY "APACHES" McCLURE and DECKER

FIRST JAP LANDS, AND
TAXIES TO WAITING C-54's

EMISSARIES LEAVE
BETTY BOMBER
GO TO C 54

INSTRUCTIONS FROM GEN. THOMAS

THEN IT'S ON TO
MANILA and McARTHUR'S
HEADQUARTERS.
— ▾ —

Stan flew a planeload of reporters over the site of the second atomic bombing and years later wrote, "Nagasaki, a hilly city, was devastated wherever it was exposed to the force of the bomb. I remember that the effects of heat were visible for miles. The metal towers for power lines, which ran on the hill tops, were shriveled."

After the Japanese surrender, flyers were no longer needed, so Stan was transferred to a military police company in Tokyo in September 1945. He got bored, returned to the States, and was discharged in December. He received the Air Medal and had flown 700 hours as pilot-in-command, 150 hours in combat.

Years after the war, Stan attended the 345th Bombardment Group's fifteenth reunion[3] and brought home a brief history card:

In 26 months flew 58,562 combat hours in 9,120 strike sorties

Dropped 58,000 bombs weighing 6,340 tons

Fired over 12,500,000 rounds of ammunition

Sank 260 enemy vessels weighing nearly 190,000 tons

Destroyed 367 enemy aircraft

Won four distinguished unit citations

Lost 177 aircraft with 580 men killed

Average life expectancy for a crew was 4.4 months[4]

After enrolling at the University of Washington under the GI Bill, Stan graduated with a bachelor's in transportation. Then Stan returned to his roots: automobiles. He teamed up with his father and brother in founding a foreign car dealership. Initially they specialized in English cars, selling Austin, Hillman, Sunbeam, Austin-Healey, Morris Minor, and MG brands.

Stan met his wife Anna Mae in college, and they wed in 1947. The two became interested in time-speed-distance road rallies and competed with Stan as driver and Anna Mae as navigator. They specialized in the newly introduced front-wheel-drive cars from England and attended rallies in the Northwest and Canada for several years. The couple raised three daughters.[5]

ANNA MAE AND STAN SHOWING OFF THEIR AUTO RALLY TROPHIES.

The auto dealership evolved. They dropped English cars, as government regulations prohibited their importation and sold Jeeps for several years, then Volvos. Between sales and service, the business employed seven people. After their father died, Stan and his brother Richard continued with the business.

Stan Trohimovich evolved too. He became disenchanted with his military participation in World War II. "We were, in effect, just a smaller scale version of the Dresden, Germany, incident in which 250,000 civilians were massacred," he said in 1987. "We were ordered to barrage the entire countryside. We may have hit some 'accidental' military targets, but most were just civilians."

On the fiftieth anniversary of the end of the war with Japan, Stan voiced his dissatisfaction in an opinion column for the local newspaper:[6]

> Not so widely known, but my bomb group became terrorists in
> April 1945, which means this was probably Roosevelt's policy.

Civilians are targets of war! We were told that everything was a target because if anyone went down, we would be killed.

Flying at 50 to 300 feet above the terrain, we were in B-25s equipped with 12 forward-firing machine guns and bombs. Terror! We spread our terror more slowly than would an atom bomb, but it was still terror. "Everything was a target" was a standing order, which we applied thereafter, mainly against Formosan civilians. There is no doubt this policy would have applied to the upcoming invasion of Japan.

However, Stan did not question the use of the atomic bomb on Japan: "I doubt that Truman imposed any more cruel policy on Hiroshima and Nagasaki than that which had been put into effect by Roosevelt, Churchill, and Stalin." He had flown his B-25 over the massive Allied naval armada awaiting the invasion of Japan, and he knew what was awaiting them.

In 1972, Stan, brother Richard, and their wives filed incomplete Federal income tax returns[8]. Instead of putting dollar amounts in the forms, they wrote comments about the US Constitution. Thus began a thirty-eight-year battle that would cost the Trohimovich family dearly. Stan became a self-taught scholar of the US Constitution and represented himself in a lonely battle against the system.

Washington State revoked his business license after he failed to pay over $20,000 in taxes. He withheld payments for business insurance premiums. Convinced the Bonneville Power Administration was overcharging the local utility, Stan withheld a portion of his electric bill and then petitioned the utility not to cut off his power. Pressed to pay overdue taxes, Stan resisted, saying it would be difficult since the country had left the gold standard. Stan argued that his customers paid him in Federal Reserve Notes, which are not lawful money and are therefore worthless. The court rebuffed him, pointing out he used these supposedly worthless notes to pay his bills.

Stan passed away in 2011 at age eighty-eight; his obituary captures his struggle:[9]

Beginning in the 1970s, he was well known on Grays Harbor for fighting local, state and federal governments, often over tax issues, and seven times was jailed for his beliefs. He owned an Aberdeen Volvo dealership, Grays Harbor Motors, until the company revoked it in 1984 after Trohimovich was sent to a federal jail for 5½ months for a contempt of court citation.

He filed dozens of suits against government agencies over the years and always acted as his own attorney, painstakingly researching his cases, producing voluminous single-spaced briefs and reveling in minor victories. He wrote hundreds of letters to the editor. He considered suing the University of Washington for fraud because of what he had been taught about the country's monetary system.

He had ultimate respect for the U.S. Constitution and maintained that every law and treaty passed since ratification of the 17th Amendment in 1919 was invalid. The amendment changed the way U.S. senators were elected, from being chosen by state legislatures to being chosen by a direct vote of the people. Since that was done improperly, he said, everything Congress did after that was nullified.

"As maddeningly single-mindedly persistent as he could be, urging me not to change one word of a single-spaced, five-page letter to the editor, Stanley J. Trohimovich was no crank," said John Hughes, former Daily World editor and publisher. "He was a man of fierce integrity, deep faith and the courage of his convictions, willing to sentence himself to 'the federal motel' if that's what it took to try and bring Uncle Sam to his senses. He was an American original.

As a matter of principle, Trohimovich refused to accept his Social Security checks for more than two decades, until financial issues made him relent in 2009.

Stan achieved immortality—of sorts. Wikipedia gives Stan credit for the fallacious tax protester's argument "that the Seventeenth Amendment to the United States Constitution was not properly ratified, and that all laws passed by Congress since the year 1919...are invalid." "Trohimovich v. Commissioner" is cited as a textbook legal brief on frivolous tax arguments, the consequences of deliberate refusal to obey court orders, and the court's inherent power to condemn and punish abusive conduct.[10]

Stan Trohimovich.

THE GREAT LIES

—∞—

In 1945 Waco '923 entered the dangerous and often lethal occupation of crop dusting.

IN 1945 WACO '923 WAS SOLD TO CENTRAL Aircraft in Yakima, Washington. Most everyone has heard two famous lies: "The check is in the mail" and "I am from the government, and I am here to help." In buying an antique biplane, be aware of a third one: "This aircraft has never been a crop duster."

CROP DUSTER OVER THE YAKIMA VALLEY IN 1944.

Many military surplus airplanes were turned into crop dusters or, to use the more sophisticated phrase, aerial applicators. Most of the planes were pretty tired after being beaten up by student pilots for years. They had little value at the end of the war since the government sold them off by the thousands. Although the open-cockpit layout was obsolete, Waco '923 lent itself well to agricultural use, having a fat fuselage for chemicals and a radial engine up front with good cooling. The instrument panel, controls, and seat for the front cockpit were removed and replaced with a chemical hopper for either dust or liquid.

> AgAir Update describes the agriculture and birth of crop-dusting in the region:[1]

> Eastern Washington, with its rough topography, is almost "wall-to-wall" wheat...The fabulous valleys of this region, especially Washington's incredibly fertile Yakima Valley, produce an abundance of almost anything that will grow. They are particularly renowned for the production of potatoes, fruits of every variety, edible beans and peas, corn, and forage crops. There are also miles of grapes, especially the Concord variety favored in the production of jams and jellies. Hops, an essential ingredient in the making of beer, grows perfectly in this region. The bulk of U.S. production of this vital crop comes from here.

> Central Aircraft began as a small flight service in 1939, quickly expanding into a training school for naval cadets during the early years of World War II. Then, in 1943, the conflict produced a critical shortage of farm labor, and Central rather quietly entered the ag flying realm with the purchase of its first ag plane, a Waco from...Arkansas.

> The Waco arrived in time to dust the extensive potato acreage during the 1943 season. From that time on, Central expanded rapidly and began concentrating on agricultural aviation...They did much to develop the acceptance of ag aviation in this region and, in 1944, did the first application of hormones in the Yakima Valley. This was an experimental job where hormones were sprayed on apple and pear orchards to prevent the fruit from dropping prematurely. The experiment worked well, and this became widely adopted practice.

CENTRAL AIRCRAFT WACO UPF-7, HEMLOCK LOOPER CONTROL
PROJECT, CLATSOP COUNTY, OREGON, 1945.

Central Aircraft would send an aircraft, pilot, and loader out to small agricultural communities. The crew would live in these little towns for the season, then fly the planes back to Yakima for maintenance during the winter. Central Aircraft eventually phased out of the agricultural application business and sold their aircraft to pilots who had been working in these communities.

SNAKES AND FIRE

—⟋ɯ⟍—

Life did not get any easier for Waco '923 when it was sold to another crop duster.
The aircraft and a sister ship were wrecked in "dusting" accidents.

IN 1955 WACO '923 WAS SOLD TO VERNE Alumbaugh of Omak, Washington. "Snakes and fire were the only two things my dad was afraid of," said Max Alumbaugh,[*] Verne's old-est son.

> As a teenager, I worked for him dusting apple orchards near Pateros, Washington. In May 1956 Dad was flying the Waco off a short airstrip on a little plateau and had counted on running off the end, then building up airspeed. This time he put in too much dust, ran the plane full throttle off the edge, descended into the ravine, bounced, then caught the landing gear in sage-brush and flipped over on its back. As the debris settled, Dad was hanging by his seat belt, looking down at a big rattlesnake on the ground just below. Meanwhile I had jumped in the pickup truck and raced down the hill to find Dad scrambling up the hill, shaking and hollering in a high-pitched voice. The landing gear folded but otherwise the airplane wasn't torn up too bad.[1]

Verne Alumbaugh was born in Kansas in 1919, served in the navy during World War II, and settled in central Washington with his wife and four children. After Central Aircraft dissolved, there was plenty of demand for crop-dusting wheat fields and apple orchards. Verne managed two airports, Omak and Tonasket, and owned several crop dusters, including two Wacos.

---

[*] Max Alumbaugh earned his aircraft mechanic's license and went to work for Boeing in Seattle. He helped bring the prototype Boeing 747 to life and stayed with the new airliner for three years as operational and maintenance procedures were worked out. He splits his time between relaxing in sunny Arizona and fishing in Washington.

Verne's business, A & M Flying Service, got off to a rocky start. His partner, Harry McSwane, took a student pilot up for unauthorized aerobatics. They were killed when the plane hit the ground near the Tonasket airport in 1955.[2] The insurance company refused to pay the claim, citing an exclusion for aerobatics, a decision upheld by the Washington Supreme Court.[3]

In 1957 Verne had a bad accident in a Waco. He was spraying an apple orchard in Brewster when he clipped a power line, just missed a school bus, stalled, and hit the ground hard upside down. Verne was thrown forcefully into the military-style seat belt and ruptured his intestines. Initially taken to the hospital in Omak, Verne was airlifted to Spokane for surgery. Verne did not fly for a year and a half. He had a wound drain in his abdomen for a year and said he had more respect for women wearing Kotex pads since he needed one during this time.[4]

One morning Verne found the plane's battery dead and hand-propped the Waco. The propeller kicked back and broke his lower-left arm. He flew again the next day with a plaster cast on his arm. While spraying an orchard, he pushed full throttle, but then his cast caught the mixture control, cutting off fuel to the engine.* Verne was too low to recover and landed in a cow pasture, hitting a fence post and breaking the lower-left wing spar.

---

* Piston aircraft engines are usually shut down by pulling the mixture control to idle cutoff, starving the engine of fuel. This minimizes the chance of fire or the engine accidently starting if the propeller is moved.

The Perry Technical Institute is a vocational technical school in Yakima that specialized in training aviation technicians during World War II. Verne shipped the wreck of the Waco there along with an employee, Gerald Climer, who needed a major project to finish up his FAA Airframe and Powerplant mechanic's license.

It was a functional restoration. The cockpit instruments were moved up to the center trailing edge of the upper wing. No crop duster pilot wishes to be looking down into a dark cockpit while flying low over the ground, so placing them up top, near the line of sight, was a big improvement. Not wanting a repeat of his accident, Verne had the mixture control disconnected. He was flying full rich at low altitude anyway and could turn the magnetos off to shut down the plane.

Recognizing the hazards of crop-dusting, Verne sprang for a major safety expenditure: a custom flying helmet costing several hundred dollars. A mold of his head was made, and the helmet was built up with fiberglass strips. Verne was very proud of his helmet and, when the plane was parked, kept it locked in the baggage compartment of the Waco, just behind the pilot's seat.

Verne flew back to Omak after a day of spraying and pulled into his parking spot. He turned the magnetos off as he pushed the throttle wide open to shut the engine down. The engine kicked back, which was not unusual. He tied down the wings and tail and locked his helmet in the baggage compartment. As Verne walked away from the aircraft, he heard a crackle and a sputtering sound and turned back. A tiny stream of flaming gasoline was dripping from the exhaust—something had hung up in the carburetor mechanism. He tried to put the fire out by blowing on it, then digging and throwing dirt on it. He was a long way from the hangar, and there was no one around to help out.

The fire spread and consumed the Waco, reducing it to a bare frame. Worst of all, it took Verne's helmet with it—he was flustered and could not remember the code to the combination lock. He never ordered another helmet.

Verne's ambition extended beyond airport management, crop-dusting, organizing a flying club, and training pilots. West Coast Airlines served the Omak airport but pulled out in 1961, having averaged only 2.2 passengers per day. Verne envisioned twice-daily shuttle service between Omak and Wenatchee to connect with West Coast's network.

Expecting a booming business for the 1962 Seattle World's Fair, Verne paid $12,500 for a twin-engine military surplus Beechcraft C-45H. His sons stripped out hundreds of pounds of old radios and wiring to turn it into an eight-passenger airliner, and Verne applied to the Civil Aeronautics Board for approval as a feeder airline.[5]

FATHER AND SON INSPECT THEIR TWIN BEECH AIRLINER.

Sadly, the airline would not last. The Beechcraft developed a rough running starboard engine, and Verne moved the aircraft for maintenance. In a local newspaper he recounts the events: "I was taxiing to the hangar, and when I tried to use the brakes to turn the plane, they wouldn't hold. I saw I was headed right for the gasoline fuel pumps and started chopping every switch in sight. The instant the left engine hit the fuel stand, it burst into flame. I went back through the cabin so fast I don't remember getting out of the seat."

VERNE RACED TO THE ANCIENT FIRE ENGINE HE KEPT IN A GARAGE AT THE AIRPORT.
"GOING BACK TO THAT PLANE WAS THE HARDEST THING I'VE EVER DONE."

All that gasoline was burning, and we'd recently filled the tanks. I had to really force myself to get close to it." He and son Max cranked up the pumper but soon ran out of water. It did not matter, since magnesium components of the engine had caught fire. Water makes a magnesium fire burn hotter and can cause an explosion since the heat separates the water into hydrogen and oxygen. Several fire trucks arrived and prevented the fire from spreading to the gasoline pumps and storage tanks.

VERNE'S BEECHCRAFT, ONLY PARTIALLY COVERED BY INSURANCE,
WAS REDUCED TO A SMOLDERING PILE OF METAL.[6]

Both of Verne's Wacos had been wrecked and retired to the scrapyard. He began crop-dusting in Piper Super Cubs. To conform to a new regulation, Verne installed fire extinguishers on the ceiling of the baggage compartment, just behind the rear cockpit.

Tragedy struck the Alumbaugh family in September 1962. Up near the Canadian border in the Pasayten Wilderness lies a beautiful area called Horseshoe Basin. No motorized vehicles were allowed, but Emmett Smith, a sheepherder, had permission to fly in supplies for his flock. Deer hunting was good, but you needed an excuse for flying—not hiking or riding a horse—in. Verne arranged to fly two planes in with salt for Smith's sheep and then do some hunting.

As they headed home, Verne and his mechanic took off in the first Super Cub. Howard Verbeck,[*] twenty-nine, a crop duster pilot who had worked for Verne for a year, flew the second Super Cub with Marvin Alumbaugh, Verne's fourteen-year-old son, in the back. Shortly after departure, the plane's engine quit. According to the local newspaper, "Alumbaugh looked back to discover Verbeck's plane was missing. He turned his craft to see the Super Cub losing altitude, heading east instead of west. The plane crossed a ridge and went out of sight. Alumbaugh followed. During the brief period the two planes were separated by the ridge, Verbeck fought a losing battle."

A deputy sheriff pilot, later sent to the scene, commented: "A steep hillside was the only possible landing spot. There was a narrow clearing about 180 yards long. At the bottom, towering up into the clearing and cutting short the available space, was an aspen thicket."

Howard headed for this opening, was forced to cross the aspen thicket high, then attempted to flare on the rocky, forty-five-degree slope. The plane hit hard, and with the sudden stop, the fire extinguisher broke loose, hitting Marvin in the back of the head, killing him instantly. His seat belt broke, and he was thrown clear of the wreckage. Howard suffered a compound leg fracture, skull fracture, and lacerations and was thrown partially out of the cockpit. He had enough strength to wave feebly at Verne as the worried father circled overhead and watched hopefully for a sign of life. On the second circuit, Verne saw Howard's arm move.

Verne raced to a nearby landing strip and set the rescue in motion. He recruited a local helicopter pilot to fly a surgeon to a clearing near the crash scene. The US Forest Service had eight smokejumpers parachute to the crash site. They moved Howard downhill by stretcher, with a bone sticking out of his torn pant leg.

Horseshoe Basin is seven thousand feet above sea level, and the Bell crop duster helicopter could not develop enough power to depart with Howard on board. A military fire rescue Kaman HH-43B helicopter was sent from Fairchild Air Force Base. The landing zone was tight, and the main rotor blades of the two helicopters just nicked each other. The damage was minor, and both aircraft were deemed airworthy. The air force helicopter carried Howard to a hospital with the doctor and then retrieved the deputy sheriff with Marvin's body.[7]

Verne was plagued with guilt over having installed the fire extinguisher in the Super Cub. He felt he had contributed to his son's demise. His wife Wilma did not want Howard Verbeck flying for them anymore, so he left to find other crop-dusting work.

---

[*] Howard Verbeck was a high school athlete, college track man, and rodeo bulldogger. He began his career as a smoke jumper, served in the 101st Airborne Division, and later learned to fly. He survived seven aircraft engine failures and crop-dusted for thirty-eight years all over the western United States before becoming a long-haul trucker in his seventies. He subsequently retired in Idaho and currently helps out as a truck driver.

The wings of the crashed Super Cub were removed and left in the woods, while the fuselage was pulled five miles down a trail by a horse and five men, led by Verne's son-in-law, James Walter. The cause of engine failure was not found.

Somewhere up in Horseshoe Basin, Pasayten Wilderness, near the Canadian border, a couple of Super Cub wings are rotting and rusting out, melding with the forest floor. Horseshoe Basin features some of the most beautiful meadows in Washington state and has become a popular hiking area. Sheep or cattle are no longer grazing, and aircraft are not allowed to land.

HORSESHOE BASIN

Verne Alumbaugh's luck as a pilot ran out in September 1963 at age forty-three. Max said, "My Dad should not have been flying on that day. He was recovering from flu or pneumonia, and was depressed over Marvin's death the year before. Even though I had gotten my commercial pilot's license, he would not let me do any crop-dusting. Plus, he was under pressure from customers during harvest season to get the work done."

Max was flagman, marking the passes over the wheat, as his dad made several runs in his Super Cub. During a turn Verne's wingtip clipped the top of a hill, the plane bounced twice, cartwheeled, and crashed nosefirst, its fuel tanks bursting into flame.

Max pushed through the wheat field to find the fire mostly burned out and a skeletal airframe. "I couldn't see my dad; the cockpit was empty. He must have slid underneath, but I knew he was gone."[8]

AN AMBULANCE ATTENDS VERNE'S FATAL CRASH SITE. [8]

Max headed for home, twenty-five miles away, stopping by to pick up the family doctor. They broke the news to his mother, and the doctor gave her a shot of sedative. Verne's customers had counted on his crop application during this busy season, and Max scrambled over the next two weeks to find other crop dusters to take care of them. "Snakes and fire were the only two things my dad was afraid of," said Max.

The days of Waco '923 as a crop duster were over.

THE TOOTH CARPENTER

—∭—

In 1961 two Waco wrecks were rescued from the scrap yard.
Two years of painstaking labor brought them back to life like new.

JACK FOWLER WAS BORN A FARM BOY SOUTH of Spokane and paid for college with money he made as a night janitor. Toward the end of World War II, the Army Air Forces needed dentists more than it needed pilots. It paid Jack Fowler's dental school tuition at Washington University in St. Louis. He left the air force as a captain and opened his own practice in 1949. It lasted fifty years.[1]

A buddy from dental school took Jack flying. It piqued his interest, and he received his private pilot's license in 1959. A friend was building a Great Lakes biplane, and Jack decided to tackle a project himself. Jack wanted a biplane too and had heard that a scrapyard in Yakima had crop duster wrecks. Their condition was poor:

WACO '923'S NEGLECTED FRONT COCKPIT FRAMEWORK LIES IN THE SCRAPYARD.

REAR COCKPIT.

ENGINES.

In January 1961, he paid $750 for Verne Alumbaugh's crop duster wrecks. A Spokane newspaper quotes Jack:[2]

> "The upshot was that I got some old Waco parts: two fuselages, two engines, ten sets of wings, a pile of junk. People thought I was nuts—the fabric was rotted off the frames and you couldn't see any metal for the rust."

JACK'S BASKET CASE OF WACO PARTS DEPARTS FROM YAKIMA TO HOME IN SPOKANE.

Time, patience and about $2,000 from the family bank account turned the trick. Fowler put countless hours into the project. He made one airplane from the two hulls; the work required his flying several times to make patterns for wooden parts from existing—and flying—Wacos. Armed with maintenance, operation and service manuals, he took the best parts from his two engines and made one good one; that phase took only about four months.

JACK FOWLER.

The work was done at the airport, Fowler's garage and in a rented warehouse. The airplane started to resume its original shape and was completely recovered with fabric material; work on the wings included the highly difficult "rib-stitching" phase that Fowler prefers not to dwell on. "That part just about drove us out of our minds," said Fowler. "But the whole job was a challenge—I can remember working half a day just getting the nut on one bolt in a very inaccessible place. I even did the spray painting, and I don't know anything about that."

The reconstruction took more than two years. Old planes such as the Waco were starting to be valued as fashionable classics, so a new front cockpit with a two-seat bench appeared where the crop duster's chemical hopper had been. As completion drew near, Jack took four months of dual flight instruction in another Waco UPF-7. In November 1963 he flew his very own Waco, tail number changed from NC29923 to N500PF, painted orange—Jack's favorite color.

Ye Old Orange Crate, after the Waco's painstaking reconstruction.

Jack was soon doing aerobatics in his Waco and took up anyone who wanted a ride. One day two Catholic nuns who were dental patients expressed a desire to go up. Jack took them up for the ride of their lives.

One thrilled sister asked, "What do you call it?"

Jack replied, "Waco."

The sister said, "I felt like I was in a wooden orange crate flying through the air." The aircraft was named *Ye Old Orange Crate* on the spot.

Jack decided to streamline the Waco by adding the engine cowling from a Cessna AT-17 "Bamboo Bomber." An FAA inspector informed Jack that, for the Waco to receive an airworthiness certificate, he had to fly it solo for an hour, including a dive to the

Waco's redline airspeed of 170 miles per hour. Even with the new cowling and pointed down in a steep dive, he couldn't get close to that airspeed—too much drag.[3]

Dorothy (Thompson), Jack's wife, was born in 1926 to a low-paid copper miner.[4] Times were tough in the Great Depression, and her parents turned Dorothy and her brother over to a home for children in Butte, Montana. After their mother came to retrieve them when Dorothy was twelve, the family moved to Monterey, California, and remained poor, as their mother toiled in a fish cannery. After high school, Dorothy spent a year studying art at San Jose State University, after which she got married. She and her first husband moved to Spokane in 1949 and started a family. She worked as a medical secretary. Her marriage was difficult and ended in divorce.

In 1961 Dorothy went to work for Jack Fowler, and they married in 1966. Between them, they already had six children from previous marriages. They bought forty acres of land on the west side of Spokane. On it, they built their house, a grass strip, and a hangar for five airplanes, including a workshop. Jack flew to work every day, weather permitting. This private airport is on the aeronautical charts as Fowlers NW 40 (12WA).

FOWLER'S AIRFIELD, JUST SOUTH OF SPOKANE INTERNATIONAL, HAS A SINGLE GRASS RUNWAY.

In her letter, Dorothy writes:,

> While he was learning to fly and rebuilding his first airplane, he had a dream of developing a ski area. On a five-hour drive back from skiing in Whitefish, Montana, he spotted a mountain basin full of snow near Sandpoint, Idaho, and thought, "Why should I drive all the way to Whitefish when I can ski in my own backyard?"
>
> The next day Jack rented a plane and took an architect friend over the site—it looked promising. They formed a partnership and bought a section of land in the mountains that did not have road access. They formed a corporation, sold stock, and three years later in 1963 the Schweitzer Mountain Ski Area opened with one chairlift and a lodge. Today it is one of the top ten ski areas in the U.S. and looks like a small city.[5] At age 87, Jack skied the winter before his death in 2009.
>
> Jack could not get the love of building airplanes out of his head, so he restored a Piper J-3 Cub and painted that orange too. The first year we were married I read a book while Jack did the flying, but I soon figured out that if I was going to be happily married to this man, I had better join him in his passion for flying. I learned to fly in the J-3 Cub on our 1,200-foot grass strip in 1967. Jack next built the remaining Waco parts into a second UPF-7 and sold the plane to a man who wanted it badly. He refused any dual instruction, saying he was experienced in the Waco, and promptly wrecked it on takeoff. The Waco was hard to handle on the ground and consequently I never flew it. We traveled to many fly-ins on the West Coast and picked up many plaques for "Best Waco" and "Best in the Show."

Dorothy had a strong interest in arts and crafts. In 1979, she took a pottery class, but she quickly gravitated toward sculpting. The Fig Tree online newspaper expands:

> **Dorothy was 55 years old** when the public was first introduced to her work. During an art show at Spokane Falls Community College, Dorothy exhibited the first piece she ever cast—a small sculpture of a mother holding a baby."

HEARTBEATS

You came into my life softly,
like fluttering wings
safe beneath my heart.

Holding you now in sweet embrace,
we create tomorrow's memories
you and I, only one heartbeat apart.

—Dorothy Fowler

Although she majored in art at San Jose State University as a young woman, Dorothy didn't spend much time in the studio until the early 1980s, after rearing six children.

"Caring for my family was just as important as my career," she said.

"I had a lot to learn," said Dorothy…"I also set a high goal. I set my mind to become a nationally known female artist. I wanted to show my daughter and granddaughters that they could do anything at any age if they work hard and set their mind to it"…

THE AVIATOR. 1928 KINNER ENGINE, SENSENICH PROPELLER.

In 2005, Dorothy unveiled an 8-foot, 600-pound bronze sculpture of Michael P. Anderson, the Spokane astronaut who died aboard the Space Shuttle Columbia two years before. The memorial, located outside the Spokane Convention Center downtown, captures the spirit of a man who was known for his faith, humility and service to others.

MICHAEL ANDERSON PERISHED WITH OTHER CREW MEMBERS AS SPACE SHUTTLE COLUMBIA WAS DESTROYED DURING REENTRY.

Before embarking on the project, Dorothy spent time talking to Michael Anderson's family, others who knew him and the committee that commissioned the statue. She decided on a pose that depicts Michael on bended knee with one hand holding his space helmet and the other releasing a dove of peace. The kneeling position represents humility, she explained; his uplifted arm and gaze toward the heavens portray his faith, and the dove symbolizes inspiration.

Meanwhile, Jack became a dealer for Maule Air, a family-owned business that builds light single-engine aircraft with short takeoff and landing characteristics, ideally suited for the back country and rough, unimproved airstrips. They have a big engine and big wing, climb fast, and stall slow. He sold about a dozen aircraft.

Dorothy's letter continues:

There was one more thing Jack managed to do in his busy life.

Calling himself "The Tooth Carpenter," he volunteered for missionary dentistry in Guatemala, flying our Maule airplane into jungle strips for a month at a time to relieve pain, with me assisting him. As Jack liked to say, "I've flown from the Bering Sea to the Panama Canal, from the West Coast to Nova Scotia, and all the places in between." We have been very fortunate to realize our dreams.

Boeing commissioned me to make a bronze stature of the Princess Mother of Thailand, the present king's mother. When it was unveiled in the palace in Bangkok, Jack and I were presented to the royal family. We were taught how to bow and shake the royals' hands. Jack was as comfortable with royalty as he was sleeping under the wing doing missionary work in the jungle.

Jack had one more airplane to build. He always said he was going to build his wife an airplane. He chose the plans of a Marquart Charger, a lightweight biplane resembling a Pitts Special. When finished, he had an artist put my logo on the side. It was a delightful little plane, and we flew it many hours. Jack restored or built nine aircraft.

DOROTHY AND JACK FOWLER WITH HER MARQUART CHARGER.

Jack flew the Waco 540 hours over thirteen years and sold it to Mike Cirone in 1974. Mike was not used to mountain flying and asked Jack to bring the Waco over the Rocky Mountains and deliver it in Butte, Montana. Arriving there, he found Mike had brought his wife and didn't even have a coat. Jack gave Mike his coat, exclaiming, "It was cold up there!" Mike was not interested in an extensive checkout in the aircraft, and off he and his wife went toward Ohio. Jack heard in a subsequent phone call that the airplane was dinged on the first landing.

SUNSET STRIP

—ɯ—

After years in the Pacific Northwest, Waco '923 crossed the Rockies
and made her way East to Ohio.

MICHAEL AND JUDY CIRONE MET IN GROUND SCHOOL and later married; they were both study-ing for their commercial pilot licenses. Mike's day job was as a tool-and-die repairman with Ford Motor Company, and he had a passion for aviation. They bought thirty-five acres in Ohio, cleared the land, and built a 2,500-foot grass runway, naming it Sunset Strip. They raised children who lived around airplanes as many would around cars. The airport thrived, and the parking tie-downs were full. Mike turned his hands-on skills to rebuilding airplanes. He wanted an open-cockpit biplane, but nobody would let him fly theirs...so he had to buy one.[1]

The buyer and seller of Waco '923 have differing recollections of the transaction. Judy remembers that Jack flew the Waco over the worst of the Rocky Mountains to meet them at Butte, Montana. After a checkout consisting of one takeoff and one landing, Jack told Mike, "You're great, go ahead and go."

Mike and Judy turned east for Marlboro, Ohio, nearly two thousand miles away. She remembers buzzing low to clear antelope off the runway at an airport in Montana. "The Casper airport had five windsocks, each pointing in a different direction," Judy remembers. "We rocked from one wheel to the other, and then scraped a wingtip. It re-ally didn't hurt the plane much and so we kept going. Mike was a good pilot and did well considering his short checkout. We had only basic instruments in the Waco, so we fol-lowed highways and railroads home. The weather was good, and the trip took six days. When we arrived at some airports, people took us home for the night at their house."

Their route took them through Billings, Montana; Casper, Wyoming; North Platte, Nebraska; Des Moines, Iowa; Rock Island, Illinois; and Fort Wayne, Indiana.

Mike sold the Waco in about a year, but his love affair with open biplanes train-ers didn't end. He owned several antique models: Stearman, Fleet, Tiger Moth, and Meyers. Mike and Judy owned the airport for thirty years. Then aviation slowed down. The tie-downs weren't full anymore; ultralight aircraft were more common—flying as they knew it had gotten too expensive and too regulated for many. The Cirones live in sight of the airport and are ever enthusiastic about flying. Years later Mike had a stroke and no longer flies. Even with impeded speech, Mike's love of the open cockpit is evident.

MIKE AND CHILDREN WITH THE WACO.

EAST TO NEW ENGLAND

—⁓—

The colorful White Mountains of New England beckoned as Waco '923 was put to work as a sightseeing workhorse for scenic rides.

WYLIE APTE JR. WAS BORN IN NEW HAMPSHIRE in 1934 with aviation in his blood. His father was a seasoned pilot, having flown with the US Army Air Service during World War I. His son's obituary captures his illustrious career:[1]

> [He joined] the U.S. Air Force as a second Lieutenant in 1956. Wylie was assigned to the Strategic Air Command 306th Bomber Wing at McGill Air Force Base in Tampa, Florida flying KC-97 mid-air refuelers. He did duty protecting the "Dew line" in cold war operations and spent time on temporary duty at Newfoundland, Labrador and Greenland. His last tour of duty was in the Azores, Spain and England. He helped evacuate planes from McDill Air Force Base to Ohio in preparation for a major hurricane in 1960. Following his tenure with the Strategic Air Command, Wylie was active in the Air Reserve based in New Hampshire...where they conducted air supply operations to the Caribbean islands as far south as Venezuela in response to the Cuban Missile Crisis.

WYLIE APTE JR. AT THE CONTROLS OF A USAF DOUGLAS C-124 GLOBEMASTER.

Wylie spent time working with his father and giving flying lessons at the White Mountain Airport. He was then recruited as a captain for Trans World Airlines that was then flying a civilian version of the KC-97. His group went straight to the TWA international routes because of his experience in the Azores and abroad. He was based out of New York and flew internationally. During his tenure with TWA, Wylie was involved in shuttling troops to and from Vietnam…

Wylie Apte Sr. founded the airport as a fixed base barnstorming operation to give scenic airplane rides over the White Mountains around 1934…Wylie Jr. assumed control of the airport in 1970 after his father's death. His dream was to build a thriving municipal airport in the valley that would further the prosperity of North Conway [a town in New Hampshire]. He devoted his life to the White Mountain Airport and aviation. At the height of its operations, the airport based a fleet of five restored World War II Waco UPF-7s, a Blanik sailplane, two helicopters, and four fixed wing aircraft. In the peak summer season the airport provided approximately 300 sightseeing flights allowing over 600 visitors each day an opportunity to take in the grandeur of the White Mountains from the air.

Waco '923 had not flown in a while when Wylie bought Mike's airplane. He sent a pilot to Ohio to bring the airplane back east. On the first landing in Cleveland, the pilot stepped on the brakes too hard and flipped the Waco up on its nose. Wylie flew out a replacement propeller and brought the Waco to New England. Wiley writes in a letter, "I recovered the fabric on the fuselage and retained some of the international orange color; the remainder was white with a little black trim. We named it *Peppermint Patty*. A few years later I rebuilt the aircraft, bringing it out as the *Red Baron*."[2]

A POST CARD SHOWING WACO '923, AS *THE RED BARON*, LEADING THE WAY TO THE WHITE MOUNTAINS.

There was no shortage of pilots for Wylie's operation; what better way to spend a summer day than flying open cockpit, taking passengers two at a time to admire the beautiful White Mountains? Gordon Kennington was a Waco pilot:

> I worked for Douglas Aircraft, first on ejection seats, then airframe design. Later I worked as a technical representative for Douglas aircraft in Yugoslavia. Their airline ordered DC-9's but had no money to pay for them, so they bartered with canned hams and other goods.*
>
> As a pilot I flew Ford Tri-Motors with Mayflower Airlines on Cape Cod, and Grumman Mallards with Chalk Airways in Florida. When we flew the Wacos, Wylie had green and yellow lights on hangar roof to show whether passengers were waiting. At the end of a flying season we had a big celebration dinner in the hangar. Wylie's son, John, was flying a U-control model, with stainless

---

* McDonnell Douglas's countertrade department arranged the sale of twenty-two DC-9s and two DC-10s to Yugoslavia for substantial amounts of crystal glassware, cutting tools, leather coats, and canned hams. The $3 million in canned hams that McDonnell Douglas got in trade from Yugoslavia did not sell quickly. They were finally eaten in the company's cafeteria and sold to employees.

steel wires flying in a circle outside. One of the wires broke, the model did a Cuban Eight aerobatic maneuver, then zoomed up, dragging the wires over high-tension power lines. Sparks flew and all the lights in the town of North Conway went off. Wiley asked John, "What are you going to do for an encore?"[3]

Alas, the airport was in peril, and it closed in 1988. The town had other plans for the property, and taxes shot up. Airport support money was diverted from North Conway to Fryeburg, Maine. The town provided no cost relief to plow the runway in the winter. Wylie Jr. writes, "I was the last & final owner of this airport, taking over from my father who started the airport. It was closed down after a forced sale due to being taxed out of existence by the town's greediness to raise property taxes."[4] This is a typical fate for small airports, as they tie up lots of land and generate little revenue by selling fuel and renting hangars. Private airports are usually a labor of love, and public airports are frequently a subsidized transportation hub for a municipality.

WYLIE APTE JR. AND THE *RED BARON* IN FRONT OF THE NORTH CONWAY AIRPORT HANGAR.

THE HANGAR ONCE HOUSED STORIED AIRCRAFT; NOW IT IS A SHOE STORE.

North Conway, once a quaint tourist town and gateway to the White Mountains, is now overwhelmed by outlet stores. The site of the former airport is now Settlers Green, a hotel, shopping, and dining complex.

THE FIVE UPF-7s WERE SOLD OFF, WITH WACO '923 GOING TO
LOUIS PAUL, A PILOT WHO WORKED FOR WYLIE.

I'M NEVER GOING TO DIE
IN AN AIRPLANE

—ᴍ—

Waco '923 was purchased in 1982 by Louis Paul, noted for his attraction to old biplanes,
young women and marijuana smuggling.

LOUIS JOSEPH PAUL, BORN 1919, CONTRACTED BONE TUBERCULOSIS of the shoulder as a child, and one arm became partially withered. His father was a bootlegger in Canton, Massachusetts, and his mother decided they could not care for him. At age 8, they gave him up to an orphanage as a ward of the state. Later one of his legs became infected and was shortened by 2½ inches. Louis lost touch with his parents and by age twenty-one had been trained by the state as a jeweler and watchmaker. He worked in Boston, and when the jeweler he was training under died, Louis moved to Bethel, Maine.[1]

There he met his wife, Florice, who ran a restaurant. Her parents came to love Louis after learning that tuberculosis of the bone is not contagious. According to son Eric, "He did not know he was crippled, and would climb three stories to install a television antenna." Louis Craig Paul, better known as Louie, was the couple's second son.

Referring to his brother, Eric said, "Louie's IQ was off the charts. He attended Gould Academy, a private high school, and then Maine College of Art, lasting a couple of years there. There wasn't anything he could not do. He had a good design edge, great pottery skills, and went to work as a sign painter." A local newspaper continues his story:[2]

> It took only one flight in a glider in 1973 to hook Louie, a strapping young fellow in his early thirties, to the skies. His brother, who worked for IBM, attended a seminar on gliders or "sailplanes" in Elmira, New York. Louie and his father tagged along, and each took a "glide." That one trip meant the demise of Paul's work as a florist in Portland.

"I quit my job the next day, slapped my money down and said I want to fly a glider," Paul's voice boomed with a hint of the determination and addiction he felt that day. "So, I ended up getting my commercial license that summer. Now I'm trained to fly everything except a hot air balloon." He became an instructor, and you could say he bounced around in the air currents a lot. As each airport closed, Louie flew on to another. The closer he could get to the planes, the better. "I've been on more sinking ships than most rats...I went to work on the State of Maine's Spruce Budworm Project* flying a spotter aircraft, and sprayed apple orchards for a while."

Why does a man choose to mount the double wings of an old military plane and taxi to the runway? "Well, I don't like working, for one thing." He pauses to capture his wide feelings in words. "I'd have to say the reason I love flying is because each time we go up, it's different. There are different meteorological conditions. To tell you the truth, the great outdoors is my church and mother."

After learning to fly full-size gliders, Louie developed a passion for radio-controlled model gliders. He and friends drove to the top of Mount Washington to launch their gliders and did pretty well despite severe radio interference from the powerful television transmitters on the summit.

---

* During his stint in northern Maine, Louie may have fathered his only child.

LOUIE TRAVELED TO HAWAII TO FIND SUPERB SOARING CONDITIONS FOR
FULL-SIZE AND RADIO-CONTROLLED MODEL SAILPLANES.

Brother Eric continues, "Louie was either screaming along in fifth gear or sleeping on the couch. He flew ultralight aircraft but had a couple of close calls. In Florida his engine seized, and he skipped off a swimming pool before crashing on the other side. He had another engine seizure in Maine and quit ultralights cold turkey. Once, his beat-up Subaru station wagon died on the road at the top of Pinkham Notch, New Hampshire. He removed the license plates, pulled out his hunting rifle, and—*Boom! Boom! Boom!*—filled it full of holes. Stories of a gangland killing circulated, but Louie was never identified as the owner."

LOUIE PAUL.

Louie started dating Sally Rice when she was thirteen. Later his parents discovered they were living together in Portland, Maine, and did not approve. He was pressured into getting married but told his parents, "If we get divorced, you guys are responsible because you crowded us into it." Sally wanted children, but Louie did not. After their divorce Louie moved back in with his parents. He disappeared for a couple of months—spent working as a pilot in Brazil.

Mike Twitchell, another pilot, says, "Louie and I were married to the same woman, Sally. She was a beautiful girl with a heart of gold. She drank herself to death at age 37, just as her father had at age 47. I put her in rehabilitation two or three times, but she would go back to drinking straight vodka. Her doctor said she would rather drink than live in a sober world."

SALLY RICE PAUL.

Charlie Sprague tells another side of the story:

> Louie moved to Key West and brought the Waco. He obtained
> permission to conduct air tours there but did not follow up. He
> started a more profitable business—smuggling marijuana. As a
> load came in from Central America, he would buy a brand-new
> Ford or Chevy, pull out all the interior panels, and pack the emp-
> ty spaces with four to five-hundred pounds of product. Louie
> would hire an unwitting driver to deliver the car to Maine and
> leave it in a hotel parking lot near the Portland airport. Louie
> would sell most of the marijuana to two or three customers, mak-
> ing a big profit, and keep the new car.

Louie had great parents; his father was a pretty wired-up guy, and his mother was wicked smart. They ran a little store in Bethel, and Louie used a pool table in the basement for weighing and sorting packages of marijuana. His mother kept the books for the business.

He made thousands and thousands of dollars in cash—this is what afforded him his lifestyle, buying airplanes and trips to Hawaii. I can say this because most everyone is dead now except Eric, who did not get along with his brother. Louie made one trip from South America, flying cocaine from Columbia to Miami. He made a hundred grand, but it scared the livin' daylights out of him, and he never tried it again. After making a pile of money, Louie got out of the marijuana business without being arrested

CAPTAIN LOU OVER THE WHITE MOUNTAINS.

After 2½ years of negotiation with the city fathers, state aeronautics board, and FAA, he set up a scenic air tour operation in Gorham, New Hampshire, but could not store aviation gasoline there since the airport was close to the river. He promoted his business as "Loopin' Louie" or "Captain Lou."

LOOPIN' LOUIE PULLING WACO '923 INTO THE VERTICAL PORTION OF HIS NAMESAKE MANUEVER.

He chose Bethel, Maine, seventeen miles to the east, as a hub to hangar the Waco and buy gas. Pilots who knew Louie well called him the "Scud King." When the clouds were low, Louie would ferry the plane back and forth just over the Androscoggin River. Knowing where all the power lines and bridges were, he learned to pop up out of the river at a certain pine tree, but once, he cut it pretty close. He clipped the tree and landed, denting the Cessna 140 near its wingtip. When probed about his flying by his brother, Louie said, "I'll never die in an airplane."

LOUIE AND HIS SIGHTSEEING PASSENGERS SHOW THEIR DEEP RESPECT FOR THE PHOTOGRAPHER.

Roger Guilmette, the public works director in Gorham, helped Louie get the scenic ride business up and running. To publicize his new business, Louie wanted to put the Waco on a trailer surrounded by girls in bikinis and pull it in the July 4th parade. The city council said no, so he asked if he could fly over the parade. Again, they said no, but Louie was undeterred. He installed a smoke system in the Waco and took Roger up for its first test. When Louie flipped the switch, the front cockpit filled up with smoke as Roger hollered, "I can't breathe, shut it down." They landed, Lou fixed the problem, and he flew over the parade, trailing smoke, with no repercussions.

Louie asked Roger, "Have you been under the Gilead Bridge?"

Roger said, "Sure, when fishing."

"Nah, I mean flying," replied Louie. "There's plenty of room."

Roger remembers, "Well, down we went, like threading a needle—the closer we got, the smaller the gap looked. Under the bridge we went, and I could count the rivets just above my head. Louie loved to buzz people—he liked to fly low, but not high. Sometimes if he couldn't sleep, he'd get up in the middle of night and go flying."

THE GILEAD BRIDGE OVER THE ANDROSCOGGIN RIVER.

Roger Dunham, another Waco enthusiast, remembers the man well:

Louie was one of those friends in life that you meet and cherish right away because somehow you know there won't be many more like him coming your way. When I first saw Louie and the Waco, it was 1980 or so. We were on downwind leg for the long runway at the Waco fly-in in Hamilton, Ohio. He was spiraling down at a great rate, midfield on the far side of the runway in an attempt to warn a fellow Waco pilot of a bad choice in runways—grass, yes, but too short and downhill. Without a radio, his only option was to try to scare him off by descending like a hawk about to strike.

Unfortunately, the fellow was concentrating so hard on the landing, he didn't notice the red Waco's attempt to warn him. When all else failed, Louie whipped out a camera, focused, and captured the accident on film. Steady, cool and versatile, he always made the best of a bad situation. That was Louie. We became fast friends and flew home to New England wing-to-wing. As a glider instructor, he could milk those air currents and make that UPF-7 fly as fast and far as our more streamlined cabin Waco.

"DURING THE YEARS WE RAN THE CANDLELIGHT FARMS AIRPORT IN CONNECTICUT, IT WAS NOT UNCOMMON TO SEE LOUIE POP OUT OF NOWHERE FROM BEHIND A HANGAR IN A BLAST OF SMOKE AND NOISE."

"Louie always had a beautiful girl in the front cockpit and a box of fantastic fireworks in the baggage compartment. He brought this cute doll back from South America for our two-year-old daughter."

A former housemate, Alana MacDonald, remarked, "Arrogance and willpower were Louie's trademark. Louie didn't give a frig about anybody but himself. He'd spread his money around, but as far as feelings go—he was selfish."

To call Louie a lady's man would be to give him insufficient credit. He preferred very young ladies and was dating high school students as he approached age forty. Former girlfriends grow wistful thinking back about their relationship:

"Louie tried to get me to wing walk on the Waco. We were together five or six years. He was the love of my life," says Mary Chapman. "Louie and I flew all over in the Waco, Cessna 140, L-19 and sailplanes. We moved from Maine to Key West. I waitressed there." What did he do? "He was a...I'd rather not say."

MARY CHAPMAN AND LOUIE PAUL.

"Louie was married to Sally, one of my best friends," Mary relates. "Sally had an affair with Mike Twitchell, who was another pilot—he and Louie flew together on the Maine budworm spray project. Sally later married Mike, but Sally drank herself to death. Later I ended up with Michael after Sally died. I'm not with Mike anymore, I'm with another man who I love very much. Louie used to tell me, 'There's thin line between love and hate.' Every time he cheated on me, he would say it. Some people think Louie is still alive, living in Rio."

In July 1988 Louie was on the way to the Maine coast in his Shelby Mustang to attend his nineteen-year-old girlfriend's birthday party. The road was slick with new pavement, the car did not have radial tires, and Louie came around a corner too quickly. He lost control and slid under a lowboy trailer carrying a road grader. The roof of the Mustang peeled back, and Louie was decapitated. The police speculated that alcohol might be a factor, but the last person to see Louie said he was sober, and the liquor was boxed up, unopened in the trunk. His first wife, Sally, appeared at Louie's funeral badly jaundiced with yellow eyeballs; she died a month later. Louie was cremated, and his ashes were spread from a plane flying over the peak of Mount Washington. He left behind eight aircraft, including a tow plane and several gliders in Colorado; plus a Cessna 140, Cessna L-19 Bird Dog, and Waco '923 in Maine.

Deborah DiPhilippo was Louie's last girlfriend. She recalls him fondly:

> I was waitressing in high school, and we met when I was sixteen. He took me for a plane ride—I puked in the plane after he stalled, and after landing, he asked me what I wanted to do next. I said, "Let's go dancing," and we danced all night. He was a pretty special dude; nobody was nicer. He'd pick me up from school, we would drive out into a field of flowers and sit on the roof of his white Chevrolet SS Monte Carlo listening to a tape of Bruce Springsteen and The E Street Band. He took me on vacation to Rio de Janeiro and Hawaii, where he had worked as a glider pilot. We broke up for a while, and then he wrote me a twenty-page love letter; it was the best thing I've ever found in a mailbox. I read it out loud with my girlfriends, and we all cried. I can't believe it got lost; I wanted my daughters to read it.
>
> I was a freshman at the University of Southern Maine and he was driving to my nineteenth birthday party when he died. He had a case of champagne in the trunk. I was in a daze at his funeral; later that day his dad gave me Lou's birthday present from his car trunk—a big stuffed animal with a bottle of perfume around

its neck. I kept the stuffed animal for years until it fell apart. Lou's parents bought me a kitten and took great care of me after the accident. Looking back, I don't think the twenty-year age difference would have worked out, but he was a great guy.

DEBORAH DIPHILIPPO TIES HER SHOE ON WACO '923.

In Memory of Louis Craig Paul

November 14, 1949-July 21, 1988

Capt'n Lou

Does this guy look at home in the sky? Believe me, he was. He lived and breathed flying, and when he was flying, he was complete. In this photo we are flying south just after leaving the North Conway NH Airport. I am in the front cockpit of his 1939 Waco UPF-7 open cockpit biplane. His pride and joy.

I BARELY MADE IT THROUGH
HIGH SCHOOL

—ɯɯ—

Life has been too easy for Waco '923... it will be wrecked again, this time on a mountainside
in New Hampshire. All three occupants were able to walk away.

STAN PARKER IS DESCENDED FROM A LONG LINE of industrious Parkers. He is the sixth generation to live in Littleton, New Hampshire. His great-grandfather founded the Saranac
Buck Glove and Mittens Company in 1866. Stan related, "My father was very 'English'—
he never went outside without a coat and tie on. He always stood up in shirtsleeves
and served dinner, then put his coat back on before sitting back down at the table. He
owned the pharmacy in town, but he never pushed me. He knew the drugstore business
wasn't for me."

Stan drove a taxicab and saved his tip money. He started flying at age sixteen in a
Piper J-3 Cub, paying eight dollars an hour for the plane and instructor. After time in
military service as a mechanic, he finished up his flight ratings at Embry–Riddle. With
a little over two hundred hours' flight time, Stan said, "I was towing gliders, instructing,
and pumping gas at the Lebanon, Vermont, airport when a red Twin Beech taxied in.
I told the captain I was looking for a job. Youngstown Airways flew me out to Ohio and
hired me on the spot. I was at the right place at the right time."

> Later I went to work for Lake Central Airlines flying DC-3s to
> Chicago. I was furloughed and went back to work for my dad
> at the drug store. One day an old bear of a man came into the
> store to buy a nickel newspaper. I said, "Who are you, sir?" and
> he chewed me up one side and down the other for not knowing
> him. It was Sherman Adams*, Eisenhower's right-hand man. He

---

* Adams was considered the most powerful presidential chief of staff in history and was forced to
resign over the gift of a fur coat. He was founder of the Loon Mountain Corporation, a major New
Hampshire ski resort.

gave me hell over his nickel paper, and I said, "I'm not doing this anymore."

I called Harold Buker and asked if he needed a copilot. He said he needed one the next morning: "Come on down. I'll get you a room." Next morning, we took off for Boston to pick up some passengers. On the way back the captain asked me to get coffee for them from a thermos in the tail of the Twin Beech. Back up front, I had my feet on the instrument panel as we popped out of the overcast into beautiful sunshine. I thought, this sure beats getting my ass chewed out over a nickel paper; this is what I'm going to do for the rest of my life.

Harold was a bomber pilot during World War II. He started a company in Springfield, Vermont, flying executives for several northern New England companies. I moved my wife and little boy down there. When I tried to cash my first month's paycheck, the bank told me there wasn't enough money. I was furious and drove to the airport to see Harold. He told me it was a mistake, and next day the bank had the money. Harold was an operator; he could sell anything to anybody. You couldn't help but like him. I made captain and flew five thousand hours in the Twin Beech.

Stan joined Allegheny Airlines in 1966, and it turned out to be a good choice. "While I was flying copilot, a friend at Eastern Air Lines called and said, 'You better get over here.' I said no, and years later I made captain on the DC-9, while he was out of a job.* I was very fortunate. Allegheny picked up Lake Central, Mohawk, Pacific Southwest Airlines, and Piedmont Airlines. Later when things started going downhill, I took my money and ran. I retired with two years to go, at age fifty-eight."

One day Stan flew as first officer on a US Airways DC-9 from Boston to Tampa.

The flight attendant came into the cockpit and said, "We've got a problem. A girl in the back of the airplane has taken all her clothes off, and she's running up and down the aisle." Captain Louie Demoulas unbuckled, got out of his seat, and headed

---

* Eastern Air Lines was liquidated in 1991 due to deregulation, mismanagement, high debt load, labor disputes, and a strike. A veteran observed that you are not a real airline pilot unless you have been divorced, furloughed, and your airline bankrupted. Stan has met two of the three tests.

back. He was gone a long time. I followed our flight plan and started final approach into Tampa—flying the plane, running the checklist, and handling the radio while the captain was still in back watching this girl running around with no clothes on.

The DC-9 has dual controls for flying, but not taxiing on the ground. The nosewheel can only be steered using a tiller over on the captain's side. I'm on short final, thinking, "Should I go around? I can't steer this airplane below sixty knots." Just as I landed, the captain came back into the cockpit.

We called security to meet the airplane and the flight attendants got the girl dressed. Security didn't show up, so away she went. Later I'm down in operations doing paperwork when I hear someone answer the phone: "What, there's a girl running around behind the ticket counter with no clothes on?" It turned out she obviously had a problem and was supposed to have been escorted off the flight. I wrote a lengthy report to the chief pilot, but nothing came of it.

Two weeks later I was flying another trip to Florida. A flight attendant came to the cockpit and said we had passengers onboard who had seen the memorable display. They were parents with little kids. Their five-year-old child observed, "Daddy, she's black all over."[*]

Stan started a flying business at the Franconia, New Hampshire, airport—a 2,500-foot grass strip nestled in the shadow of the Presidential mountain range. The airport was owned by the Franconia Inn and built on land acquired by Zebedee Applebee before the Revolutionary War. Because his predecessor was not paying the rent, Stan and a couple of business partners found it easy to lease the airport from the owners of the inn. Being in the mountains, it was an ideal place for flying gliders and sightseeing rides.

---

[*] In her later years, the author's mother volunteered reading aloud to students in Tyler, Texas. Many at her school were poor black kids. Just before Halloween she read a ghost story to the class. A black boy approached her after class and asked, "Mrs. Wood, are all ghosts white?" She replied, "When you're a ghost, with a sheet over your head, you can be any color you want." She received an award for twenty-five years of volunteer service.

Stan said, "We flew over to Elmira and picked up a Schweizer glider. I flew over with a tow pilot and got trained in towing gliders. He got his glider rating while we were there. When we got home, he taught me how to fly a glider, and we swapped seats. That's how I started flying gliders. It worked out okay; we didn't kill one another.

One day I heard there was a Cessna L-19 Bird Dog for sale at the Berlin airport, New Hampshire, airport. I drove up, and there in the back of the hangar was the Waco. I called my banker, and he said, "Write them a check, and we will cover it." I heard the owner had been killed in a car wreck, and his parents were selling his planes. It took quite a bit of work to get the Waco running.

Walt Lermer was an old friend of Stan's, recently retired from Allegheny Airlines. His daughter called to say her dad was getting bored and needed to do something. "She heard we were starting an airport and wanted to send him over," said Stan. "We put him in the Waco, and he had a ball with it. He flew down the interstate highway, and all of a sudden people started coming in for rides. We kept him in the cockpit all day long. My son ran to town to get sandwiches, and we fed him in the airplane. We were getting $75 for two people for a fifteen-minute ride. About dark, Walt asked, 'You fellas looking for a partner?'"

"That's what I've been waiting to hear," replied Stan.

STAN PARKER PREFLIGHTS WACO '923 AT FRANCONIA.

One day Anne Morrow Lindbergh stopped by the airport. Anne was the first licensed woman glider pilot in the United States. She sat on the porch and watched the tow planes landing downwind, hooking up gliders, and taking off upwind. "My husband would love it here," she said. "You guys don't do anything by the rules."

But the town of Littleton did not make life easy.

> We had a little sign in town that said "Airplane Rides," but they made us take it down. They would not allow off-premise signs. Even though it would be good for the motel and restaurant business, owners were jealous because they couldn't have a sign— damn fools. We wanted people to come here and stay awhile. The town selectmen came out a month after we put a sign in front of the airport.

"They said it was too big; it had to come down too. We gave up on promoting the operation."

When I took off in May 1990, there was a strong wind coming out of the west, which brings it up the side of the Cannon Mountain. On sightseeing rides I'd bring 'em around the mountain, back over the top, and then fly down the back side. There was a moose up there. I swung around so they could see it in a little bowl in the mountain. Meanwhile the wind had swung around from the east, and we got pulled down into the bowl. We later found the throttle lever bent; I had pushed forward so hard trying to get out of there.

When I saw we were going to hit the tree, I yanked back, and we stalled in. That's what saved us. We hit dead center in a birch tree, right on the prop. I hollered, "Are you guys okay?" They said, "Yeah." We sat on the top of the tree for an instant, and then the tree broke, and we went down at the nose—*boom!* I could hear gasoline dripping from the wing tanks onto the hot cylinders, going *tssh*, *tssh*. I unstrapped, got them unbuckled in the front cockpit, and we slid down to the ground. We were lucky.

WACO '923 IN A BIRCH TREE ON CANNON MOUNTAIN, 1990.

I called the FAA as soon as we got on the ground, and they asked, "What's your experience?" I said I work for US Airways, and I'm Category IIIA qualified for instrument landings.* He hung up but must not have believed me. In a few minutes, the company's chief pilot in Boston called and asked, "Are you okay?" I said sure. The FAA must not have believed me and called to see if I worked for the airline. What was this airline captain doing flying an old airplane up in New Hampshire?

Some kids were playing Frisbee and saw us crash. They drove up in a pickup and took us back to the airport. People expected us to fly back in the Waco, but here we are in the back of a pickup. My passengers said they were okay, but I insisted they go to the Littleton hospital, and we paid for it. I didn't hear any

---

* This instrument approach, designed for foggy airports, allows the aircraft on final approach to descend to fifty feet above the runway, permitting the crew to decide whether they can see the runway centerline or lights and land.

more about it, but the insurance company said there was a lawsuit brought by my passengers.

The Waco pieces sat in a hangar for quite a while. Three or four years later, I was driving north on the interstate highway, and I saw something funny sticking up out of a trailer. What the hell? It was the tail of an airplane. As it went by, I saw it was the Waco. I said to myself, "I guess the lawsuit got settled."

Two weeks after the accident, Stan got a call from the head of the New Hampshire Aeronautics Commission. He said, "Stan, they just called me, and they want me to take care of this accident. I don't see any problem; have a nice day." It was Harold Buker,* Stan's former employer.

Stan was relieved, "I never saw anybody from the state. I took care of Harold for two years, and he took care of me. Apparently, they'd had a fatal accident over in Maine the day before, so the FAA called up Harold and asked him to handle it.

About two months later, the FAA called from Portland. They said, "We see you've never had a check ride at Franconia, and we have to come over and give you one." After a flight in a Cessna L-19, the FAA inspector said, "It was a real good ride, but you didn't holler '*CLEAR!*' before you started the engine." I had just waved my hand as a signal because there was no one around. I thought he was going to bust me, but he laughed and said, "That's okay, you made it."

Reflecting back on the experience, Stan had this to say:

You know, sometimes I'd say, "I'll just sell tickets today. I've been flying four days straight, and I'm sick of it." Next thing you know, I'd be in the Piper Super Cruiser. No sooner would I get on the

* Harold Buker bought his first plane and learned to fly when he was fourteen. He enlisted at the outbreak of World War II and flew several missions as a B-24 captain in the Eighth Air Force. He was captured by the Germans after his B-24 was shot down over the North Sea, and he spent the rest of the war as a prisoner in Stalag Luft III. Buker was named the New Hampshire aviation director in 1986, received a national award for pioneering the safe use of light aircraft for commercial transportation in 1991, and in 1994 was elected president of the National Association of State Aviation Officials. He died at age seventy-seven.

ground than they would need somebody to tow a glider. Then I'd get down, and they'd need a pilot for the Cessna 180…and then a sightseeing ride in the Waco. It would go like that all day long. I'd go from one airplane to the other as fast as I could go.

I barely made it through high school. I hated school; I was always doing something else. Later, when I went to flight school, I came out at the top of the class. My high school principal moved to run a school near Boston. One day the chief pilot said to me, "I've got a new neighbor." It was my former principal.

I asked, "Does this mean I'm being fired?"

"No-o-o," he said, and we laughed. The principal probably thought I would do well if I could drive an apple truck.

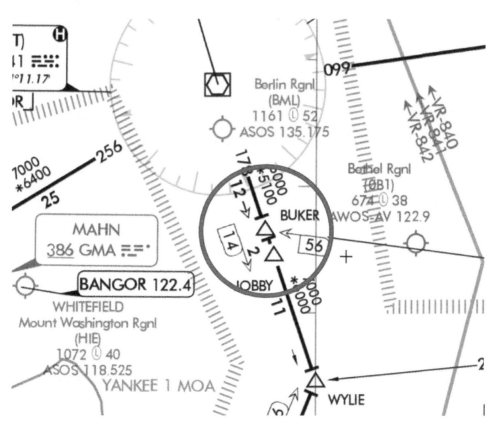

HAROLD BUKER IS HONORED WITH AN AIRWAY INTERSECTION NEAR MOUNT WASHINGTON.

Stan flew five years in corporate aviation and twenty-eight with the airlines, flying over thirty thousand hours. He is disappointed that many in the new crop of airline pilots did not learn to fly by the seat of their pants. Stan is particularly proud of Sully Sullenberger: "He has a glider rating, graduated from the Air Force Academy, and is a good speaker. We couldn't have had anybody better representing the airline industry. Sully wrote a book, made some money, and hung it up. Some other guys could have done that job, but you wouldn't want to interview them."

After Stan quit flying, he drove heavy tractor trailers for a while. Now he and his wife migrate back and forth between New Hampshire and Florida in a recreational vehicle, staying ahead of the cold weather.

Looking back Stan reflected, "That Waco is a handful of an airplane, especially on takeoff and landing. If you're landing on pavement in a crosswind, it's even tougher."

I'LL NEVER FORGET WHAT'S-HER-NAME

—◆—

Two years later, a television interview leads to a case of mistaken identity and a humorous footnote to the crash of Waco '923.

STEVE STRATFORD REACHED UP AND TAPPED HIS RIGHT eyeball with the end of a pencil—*click, click, click*—an unsettling sight and sound. His eye is prosthetic. Steve related:

> When I was nine years old, I had a hockey stick bang out my right eye. If the stick had gone a little bit further over here, I would be blind. Every day that I get up and see my toes is a good day.
>
> After the accident, doctors told me I should wear goggles that would make a welder proud—to protect the other eye. I sat down with my parents at about age eleven and said I didn't want to live like a boy in a bubble. I asked my dad how many people he knew who had lost an eye. He had served in World War II, and he named an army buddy. Then I asked how many people he knew who had lost one eye, and then later lost the other. He hesitated and said he didn't know anyone. I told them my accident was a freak thing, and there was little chance of losing my other eye. I wanted to play sports and do everything else. They were silent. Years later my mother told me they talked it over afterwards and said, "The little guy has us." I got to do what I wanted, and I still ski and play lacrosse.

Steve grew up in Lexington, Massachusetts—kindergarten to high school. While attending Boston University, Steve worked at a bar in Kenmore Square. "The pecking order was, first you worked as a doorman, then a bouncer, and then you graduated to bartender. You wouldn't believe the fights. I saw a guy break a two-by-four over another guy's head. It was quite an education for a boy from the suburbs. I found out later the bar was owned by a Mafia tough guy."

Real estate is Steve's calling—he worked days as a commercial real estate assessor while studying for his MBA degree at night. He managed Neiman Marcus's real estate portfolio for ten years. Now he is a successful senior sales associate in residential realty, right in the town where he grew up.

> Losing my eye only prevented me from doing one thing in my entire life. When I was seventeen, I went down to the marine recruiter with my best friend. We both signed up to be marines. A couple weeks later, the phone rings at home, and the recruiter talks to my dad. He said he just had a few questions about me, but my dad said, "Did Stephen tell you he's missing a headlight? He lost an eye to a hockey stick." Well, that was that. I came home from school, and my dad was mowing the lawn; he stopped and asked, "Did you think you were going to fake your way through a physical exam and training?" My friend joined the marines but never left North Carolina, so I guess I didn't miss much.

In 1990 Steve and his girlfriend were on vacation in New Hampshire. He brought his big, old, clunky video camera along to record her golf swing at a driving range. As they drove by Franconia Airport, Steve pulled over.

> He remembers, "It was a neat grass airport. They said they were giving airplane rides, and I'd never been in a biplane. I had taken some flying lessons and done skydiving but never flown in an open cockpit. I asked my girlfriend, "Are you game?" She said, "Yeah."

> I brought my video camera, and we wedged in the front cockpit and pulled one seat belt across both of us. I ran the video camera during takeoff and then on and off; it was a nice sunny day with a great view. I saw we were coming up to a ski slope on Cannon Mountain. The pilot pointed to the mountain and shouted, "Look, a moose!" over the engine noise. I held the video camera up and saw the ski lift getting closer and thought he was going to do the old bush pilot thing and skim by. Then one wing came up, and it felt like a downdraft.

> I'm looking through the viewfinder...things are getting closer and closer, and I say, "We're going in." Here come the trees, and

we go deeper and deeper into them. How we didn't get decapitated or impaled, I don't know. It was like we were floating until we got to a big white birch tree that fell over after we hit it. By the time we stopped, the tail was up in the air, and gasoline was coming out of the wing. I look back at Stan, and he asks, "Are you okay?" I checked my body parts and said, "Yes, I'm okay."

My girlfriend climbed down to the ground, and I handed down the video camera to her. Stan and I climbed down too. There was a sense of giddiness among the three of us. You just had this thing happen; we had crashed into a mountain and survived. Nobody's dead, and we are walking away, only a little banged up. Stan said, "All over that damn moose. We didn't finish the ride, so I guess I'll have to give your money back." Everyone laughed. "That's a $70,000 airplane we just destroyed. That tree saved us—to hell with the airplane, as long as no one got hurt."

STEVE STRATFORD AND HIS GIRLFRIEND CELEBRATE THEIR SURVIVAL,
AS THE WRECK OF WACO '923 HANGS IN A BIRCH TREE.

Then here comes an all-terrain vehicle up the ski slope—a crew was doing spring cleanup on the ski slope and saw us crash. One guy ran up and said, "Stan! What the hell?" Stan said, "I know." We rode down the mountain and went to the local hospital. They checked us out and released us right away. My back hurt, and the doctor said get it checked out when I got home. I didn't have any long-term problems, and neither did my girlfriend.

A year or two later, I'm watching a television show and thought they might use the video we had taken during the crash. I sent it to California and heard back from the producer that they wanted to come interview me. It came out good because they said it would be run during February sweeps week on the *Real TV* show[1]. I saw it while on a business trip and thought it was pretty funny. For years after I would hear from friends who'd seen reruns and ask, "Steve, were you in a plane crash?"

I look back on it and smile; it's been the fodder of many a joke. Friends say, "Steve is the safest guy to travel with; he's already crashed." To me it was a wonderful thing to do that ended dramatically. It was a mishap with Mother Nature and a downdraft.

My girlfriend moved to the Midwest, and about a year later, I met my wife. When the television company taped in our living room, there was no delineation between my wife, sitting next to me, and the woman in the crash video. *Real TV* assumed they were the same person. The show ran a month or so later, and my wife told me, "My mother called today. She asked if I'd seen the television show. My mother said, 'Oh my God, Lynn, I saw that video on the television show with Stephen. Did you know...?' I said, 'Yeah, I knew all about the crash.' She asked, 'Lynn, did you know he was married before you?'"

Well, I never said she was my wife, but the woman in the airplane was blond, and my wife is blond. When they edited the video, it appeared to be the same person. My wife and I laughed about this wacky experience—my mother-in-law took it all wrong."

I asked Steve about his former girlfriend, and he replied, "She worked at an architect's office here, and I approached her for a date. Her name was...uh...uh...Gosh, this is embarrassing.

"This is really sad.

"I'll never forget what's-her-name. I dated her for about a year. And...what *was* her name?"

STEPHEN STRATFORD, A LEXINGTON, MASSACHUSETTS REALTOR, SURIVIVED
THE 1990 CRASH OF WACO '923 ON CANNON MOUNTAIN.

MY GRANDFATHER'S AX

—m—

It would be three years before the wreckage of Waco' 923 found her ninth owner.
He and his partner took on the arduous task of rebuilding the plane in Massachusetts.

THE WRECK OF WACO '923 SAT IN THE hangar of Mount Washington Regional Airport while the insurance company settled and put the remains up for auction. David Frawley wanted a UPF-7; it could bring him back to his youth spent instructing in them during World War II. He submitted the winning bid, and Chris Cunningham, director of maintenance at Colonial Air in New Bedford, Massachusetts, trailered the bones to his hangar. Chris said, "We bought it sight unseen."

CHRIS CUNNINGHAM SURVEYS A "BASKET CASE," HIS WACO RESTORATION PROJECT, 1992.

Both upper and lower right wings were broken in half, and the upper center section containing the fuel tank was broken. The left wings were damaged but not as bad. We sent all five wing sections, the horizontal stabilizer, both elevators, the rudder, and vertical fin to the Shues' barn in Pennsylvania. They had the wings for the better part of a year, and I made several pilgrimages down there. Meanwhile, I was working on the airframe here and looked up Waco drawings from the Smithsonian for the welded steel tubing fuselage, the two-passenger front seat, and the engine installation.

UPPER AND LOWER WINGS ON THE RIGHT SIDE SUFFERED THE WORST DAMAGE.

Before we disassembled the airplane, we removed the broken propeller, liberated a wooden propeller from a Stearman across the field, and ran the engine. We ordered a bunch of steel tubing and replaced the whole fuselage frame behind the rear cockpit. We cut the seams, slid the old empennage out, and threw it away.

THE WACO SUFFERED ADDITIONAL DAMAGE AS IT WAS RETRIEVED FROM THE
BIRCH TREE. THE CONSEQUENCES OF WRAPPING A CHAIN AROUND THE TAIL AND
PULLING IT DOWN ARE SEEN WITH AND WITHOUT THE FABRIC SKIN.

We followed the blueprints, but it is one thing to have the draw-ings and another to see the parts together. I made several trips to the wing rebuilders to look at their airframes and take pic-tures. They had airplanes in all different states of restoration. The American WACO Club helped with sources for the engine "dishpan," curved cowlings, and an alternator replacement for the generator. The ailerons are all new; the old ones were in tough shape.

NEW SHEET METAL COMPONENTS REPLACED DAMAGED PARTS, INCLUDING THE SPUN "DISHPAN" IN FRONT.

PLYWOOD FORMERS AND SPRUCE STINGERS THAT SUPPORT THE FABRIC
COVERING WERE ADDED OUTSIDE THE WELDED STEEL TUBE FRAME.

A TRIAL FIT OF COMPONENTS SHOWS THE THE AIRCRAFT TAKING SHAPE AGAIN.

THE FUSELAGE IS COVERED WITH A SYNTHETIC FABRIC, WITH A MUCH LONGER
LIFE THAN COTTON OR LINEN USED IN THE 1940s. AFTER BEING STITCHED IN
PLACE, THE FABRIC IS SHRUNK IN PLACE WITH AN IRON OR HEAT GUN.

Dave Frawley was a funny guy, a nice guy…but he was Dave. All of
a sudden, he tells me the airplane is leaving, that someone else
is going to work on it full time and finish it up. We had taken on
the project part time, to work on it when we did not have other
business, and I would not charge David. I asked Dave, "If you are
willing to pay someone else, why don't you pay me to finish the
project?"

Okay…now the Waco is not leaving, and we are going to do it as
a job instead of a fill-in project. We are going to go at full speed.
We got to the end of it, and you can imagine how much 3,500
man-hours is worth. David said, "Well, I don't have any money;
I guess we'll just have to be partners." That was not the arrange-
ment—I did not want to be half owner of a Waco UPF-7—but
there I was.

We got to the end of it, and we had no airworthiness certificate, and we had no logbooks. The logbooks came back to us after the FAA accident investigation. I called the FAA Flight Standards District Office (FSDO) in Bedford requesting an airworthiness certificate. The FSDO was kind of a political place, and there was a lot of pushback and runaround. The FAA had a safety meeting one evening on the other side of the airport. I talked to the FAA office manager and said, "I *need* this airworthiness certificate, and I can't seem to get anywhere."

He grabbed the inspector who was dragging his feet and said, "C'mon, we're gonna go look at this." The airplane was all done and freshly painted. We turned on all the lights in the shop, and the thing almost glowed. Everything was shiny, brand new. The FAA office manager walked around the airplane slowly one time, turned to the inspector, and said, "So really, there's no reason we couldn't just issue the airworthiness certificate tomorrow, *right*?"

FRONT COCKPIT RESTORED TO ORIGINAL 1940 CONFIGURATION.

THE REAR COCKPIT IS NEARLY IDENTICAL, WITH THE ADDITION OF STARTER,
PRIMER, RADIOS, SWITCHES, AND CIRCUIT BREAKERS.

David Frawley flew the first flight, and he had someone with
him. He never flew alone. The Waco only flew about fifty hours
during the ten years we owned it. I was ready to sell the airplane
back in 1994, but Dave hung on to it. When he decided to sell
the plane, he started asking in the mid-two-hundred-thousand-
dollar range and slowly ratcheted down.

THE UPF-7 IS POPULAR AS A SIGHTSEEING AIRCRAFT BECAUSE IT SEATS
TWO IN FRONT AND HAS A DOOR FOR EASIER ACCESS.

I asked Chris why he enjoyed rebuilding and working on these old planes in addition to the business and airline jets. He replied, "The Waco is more like a homebuilt aircraft, made like a one-off, and parts are an issue. I told the wing rebuilder that we needed some brackets for the interconnect between the upper and lower ailerons. He said, 'You can't get those anymore, so we improvise.' When I came home, we made a die and then used our twenty-ton press to make a bunch of these steel brackets. I traded them for some other parts that I needed. There's no doing that for the airlines. That's all just hanging parts on the plane. When we get out on the ramp, we are just throwing parts at the problem."

This is my grandfather's ax. The wooden handle has been changed twice, and the steel head is new, but this is my grandfather's ax. The formal name of this thought experiment is the Ship of Theseus[1] or Theseus's paradox. A first-century Greek philosopher wondered if a wooden ship that had every board replaced over time would be the same ship. There are other examples of the paradox. Is a rock band whose members have all been replaced over the years still the same rock band?

After at least three restorations from a basket case, the paradox applies to Waco '923. It seems that only a few original parts remain: the welded tubular steel frame, the skeleton from the engine firewall to the aft edge of the rear cockpit, and most likely the tail control surfaces. The engine has been replaced, and it is not clear whether any original wing components survive.

GROUND LOOP!

—◊◊◊—

A World War II flight instructor sought to rekindle his youth in Waco '923.
His demise at the bottom of a stairwell raised many questions.

DAVID FRAWLEY WROTE A SHORT MEMOIR. IT MAKES clear why he wanted Waco '923:

The year was 1928 or 1929, when I took my first ride in an airplane. I was with my father when he teased me with a dollar bill at the airfield. I grabbed the dollar, went out the car window, hit the ground, flew over the fence, and ran up to the airplane. I gave the pilot the dollar bill and away we went. The pilot overshot the landing, so we had to go around again, which I thought was great since the ride was extended. The little field was in Seekonk, Massachusetts and the airplane was a Kittyhawk biplane built in Rhode Island.

Later I was going to school and working nights making $12 per week. I lived with my mother and sister and was allowed to keep $2 of the $12 I earned. I walked and thumbed out to a little field in Rochester, Massachusetts and took flying lessons 15 minutes at a time. Doing odd jobs around the airplanes, I was able to solo on December 12, 1940. The airstrip was 1,000 feet long and there were no other airports in those days other than East Boston.

One day my mother told me about an ad in the Boston Globe stating that the U.S. Army Air Corps needed pilots and an exam would be given at the Boston Armory to 1,000 applicants. My mother encouraged me to take the exam, although I doubted I would ever pass. She told me to take a chance, so I left my house at 5 AM one morning and walked to the train station in New Bedford. I took the steam engine to Boston with the money she gave me. The exam lasted from 8 AM to 4 PM, and I felt sure I did not pass because it was rather difficult.

When I came home two weeks later my mother told me I had received another letter. I thought it was a rejection, however I was one of the 400 chosen. I was to arrive at Tufts Engineering College in Medford, bringing only an army blanket. My uncle dropped me off and I took a very lonely walk down the street to the admissions office where an Army sergeant was waiting. Luckily, I was assigned a room with a George Lowe who had just graduated from MIT and we became great friends. We studied hard, often burning the midnight oil by covering our lamps at 10 PM so no one else could see the light. He came in first on the exams and I came in third, with subjects ranging from mathematics, meteorology, celestial navigation, dead reckoning navigation, cold weather operations and aircraft engines.

When we weren't going to school we went to Concord, New Hampshire to receive advanced training in Waco UPF-7 biplanes. It was very cold, and we flew on skis most of the time as it never seemed to stop snowing. George and I did well and were assigned to Northeastern University for advanced navigation, moved to Winston-Salem, North Carolina for advanced radio and celestial navigation, then to Parkersburg, West Virginia where an advanced instrument flying school was just starting. We trained in airplanes and the famed Link Trainer, the first simulator in aviation.

I instructed in the Army Air Corps until the war ended and was discharged in 1945. The wealthy owner of our newspaper wanted an airline, so his son and I started Mass Air, making runs from New Bedford to Martha's Vineyard, Nantucket and Boston. We flew Lockheed 10s, Cessna T-50s, Beech 18s, DC-3s and numerous single engine aircraft. We had an Army surplus Link Trainer, and being the first flight instructor in New Bedford, I was kept very busy.

Helicopters were new at the time and I received my commercial license in a Bell 47. The first multi-engine helicopter in the world, the Omega BS-12, was designed and built in New Bedford. It was a sky crane or utility aircraft, and I became the test pilot.

DAVID FRAWLEY AS HELICOPTER TEST PILOT IN THE MID-1950S. THE BS-12 WAS NOT A SUCCESS; FOUR UNITS WERE BUILT, AND THE PROGRAM WAS CANCELED IN 1960.

I served a chief pilot for several airlines and charter operations that started over the years and by 1980 was flying jets for executives of the Boston Red Sox. In that year I also was designated as FAA pilot examiner to administer flight tests in a wide variety of aircraft:

Douglas DC-3	Grumman TBM
North American B-25	Grumman Albatross
Boeing B-17	Lockheed Loadstar
Consolidated B-24	Hawker HS-125
Consolidated PBY	Cessna 500 Citation
Martin B-26	

Dave tested pilots for initial ratings and annual recurrent training by traveling around the United States, England, France, Italy, Switzerland, and the Netherlands, plus doing check rides in firefighting water bombers. He accumulated over thirty thousand flight hours and taught about three thousand pilots to fly. Dave worked for the New England Telephone Company for forty-one years. Dave's wife left him during the war to become a ballerina in Los Angeles. Things did not work out, and she asked Dave to take her back. He declined. Dave had no children.

The New England Escadrille, a warbird enthusiast group, acquired a Douglas C-47A, *Plunkett's Passion,* a military transport version of the DC-3. Dave Frawley was a key player in the Escadrille because he could instruct an applicant, recommend them for the check ride, and conduct the check ride in the DC-3. FAA regulations have since changed, and a separate instructor must now sign off the pilot for the check ride. The FAA suspected designated examiners of abusing the previous regulations by giving out type ratings without proper training or demonstration of proficiency.

The DC-3 was the first modern airliner and an aviation classic in its own right. The author's desire to fly this aircraft lead him to meet Dave Frawley and have his first glimpse of Waco '923, in 1997. The image of the beautiful biplane in the hangar at New Bedford stuck, but the DC-3 came first.

As one of about thirty pilots who were DC-3 type rated by Dave, I can attest that there were no shortcuts. The lessons began before you got close to the airplane. I remember Dave telling me, "John, these round engines are delicate and expensive to overhaul. You always want the engine driving the propeller and never the propeller driving the engine. Be really smooth with the throttle and prop levers, and don't close the throttles until just before touchdown."

Dave said, "You can't be a DC-3 pilot unless you have been a DC-3 copilot," so he put me in the right seat for the first two lessons. In preparation for the training, I had spent hours in the cockpit finding things and had gone over the flight manuals in detail. I listened to Dave. My first experience was humbling and hilarious. The plane had been flown by others to Hyannis, Massachusetts, for a transponder check and had been sitting for a while, and hydraulic pressure had bled down to zero.

We preflighted and strapped into the DC-3. Dave taught me the engine start procedure—our hands were flying over starter, primer, magneto switches, throttle, and mixture controls. The right engine started right up, but with no hydraulic pressure and no brakes, the plane began a tight turn to the left. This took us off the tarmac at the Hyannis ramp and onto the grass.

STARTING THE LEFT ENGINE AT NEW BEDFORD.

I reached down to the hydraulic hand pump and asked Dave, "Do you want me to pump?"

"Pump, John, pump!" Dave shouted.

Pump I did as he worked solo at starting the left engine. We made a 180-degree turn on the grass without hitting anything and lumbered back up onto the tarmac. The ground controller in the tower said not a word.

Next, I learned the steps required for raising and lowering the landing gear; operating fuel boost pumps, wing flaps, and cowl flaps; locking and unlocking the tail wheel; backing up the pilot on the throttles; setting takeoff power; and completing first and second power reductions after takeoff. With the runway behind us and the plane climbing away came the best part: we each looked out our respective side windows to check the 1,830-cubic-inch, 1,200-horsepower Pratt & Whitney engines in their nacelles swinging eleven-and-a-half-foot-diameter propellers. The expected call was "No smoke, no fluids this side."

Much of my first lesson in the left seat was spent learning to taxi. The New Bedford tower loaned us the unused Runway 14/32, and I taxied back and forth, back and forth, making S-turns, then running straight down the runway, followed by a 180-degree turn at the end. The DC-3 has a nonsteerable tail wheel, so directional control is accomplished by varying throttle settings and braking, left and right. The big vertical stabilizer makes the plane an excellent weathervane, always tending to swing the plane into the wind, and this movement is offset by differential throttles, brakes, rudder, and aileron.

The pilot has to apply extra power on the upwind side and press the opposite rudder to keep the DC-3 from turning off the runway into the puckerbrush. Considering its ninety-five-foot wingspan, you need to be situationally aware on taxiways. The tail wheel can be locked for long, straight taxi runs, takeoff, and landing. Meanwhile, the cockpit crew is holding on to the yoke to keep the wind from banging the control surfaces around.

In the air, controlling the DC-3 took large movements and some muscle. I noticed that Dave wore work gloves while flying, and soon I did too, especially if the aircraft had cold soaked overnight. The required maneuvers were preordained by the FAA, including stalls, steep turns, rejected takeoffs and landings, engine out practice, and all sorts of instrument approaches.

The old airplane had "steam gauges," so everything was flown using raw data, increasing the applicant's workload. For simulated instrument flight, the student wore a hood restricting outside vision. Dave was notorious for beating up students if he thought they weren't getting it quickly enough. I felt pretty good flying the plane and taking care of the prelanding sequence until Dave burst out over the headphones, "Damn it, John, the localizer needle is alive. Why don't you turn inbound?"

After landing and parking, the left-seater was the last one to move; mechanics and other volunteers bailed out of the plane first. On a windy New England day, you hung on tight on the controls, guarding them from sudden gusts snatching them out of your hands before external rudder, elevator, and aileron locks could be installed. Landing gear pins were inserted to keep the gear from folding after hydraulic pressure bled down.

Dave had a reputation for conducting thorough oral exams—mine lasted an hour and a half. Preparation was interesting, as it used study materials and handbooks that had been through a copy machine countless times and dated to 1945. It was said that Dave, probably like many examiners, knew whether an applicant would pass the check ride by his or her performance on the oral.

Hazing was part of the initiation into the DC-3 fraternity. On a cold fall day, the student was expected to pull a stepladder up to the trailing edge of each wing, drag a five-gallon container of sixty-weight oil up the slippery, frosted walkway, and service each twenty-nine-gallon oil tank. The oil poured like molasses. When it was my turn to undergo this ritual, the New England winds would blow light, feather-like filaments of the heavy oil off the filler neck and onto my gloves, sleeves, and pants, the clothes I was committed to for the rest of the day. I wanted to be bright and shiny getting into the cockpit but seldom felt that way.

The next step was opening two fuel caps on each side of the plane and confirming fuel on board using marked wooden dipsticks. Finally, after climbing up to the cockpit to confirm the magnetos were off, each engine had to be pulled through, by hand, at the end of a long propeller blade to ensure engine oil had not drained into the bottom cylinders, causing hydraulic lock. Of course, there were mechanics and other volunteers around the aircraft—but the applicants were expected to do their part. It was the rite of initiation to the cult of the Douglas DC-3.

THE SUPPLICANT PULLING THROUGH THE PROPELLER, CHECKING FOR HYDRAULIC LOCK.

It was good while it lasted. I paid $800 per hour, wet*, for precious hours in the venerable DC-3, an aviator's deal of a lifetime. After the check ride, when the pressure was off, eleven of us went up for a ride on a beautiful, warm Indian summer day in October 1996. The leaves around Cape Cod were at peak color. Dave Frawley shifted gears. No longer was he the hard-ass examiner; we were gathered that fabulous fall New England day to celebrate the Douglas DC-3. Tree leaves were turning brilliant gold, orange, and red below. How could we be so lucky to be aloft in the timeless DC-3 that morning?

My after-takeoff duties were completed, we climbed to 1,200 feet, and were rumbling along. I looked out the left side to see the big propeller thrashing away. I unbuckled, got out of the left seat, walked back to the cabin, and asked my wife to take my place. Seating her in the captain's seat, Dave had her make mild turns in each direction, and then she stepped up, back, and out to let other pilots onboard take their turns. When she returned to my side, my wife reported, "It is like flying an apartment building," Then again, I don't think any of us, except Dave, knew what it was like to fly heavier piston airplanes, such as the B-24, with unboosted controls.

THE AUTHOR WITH DAVID FRAWLEY AFTER THE DC-3 CHECK RIDE.

---

* In the flight vernacular, "wet" means the hourly rental cost of the aircraft includes fuel.

An indelible memory of DC-3 training persists. While I was preparing for the check ride, Dave told me, "You fly for a while, but then I have two annual recurrent check rides to get done. They are both senior airline captains who also fly the B-17, B-24, and C-47 in the Confederate States Air Force. You can take a break while they fly." This seemed fine to me; I had never ridden in the back of the airplane with someone else flying, and a break to watch and learn from the pros would be good. We went round and round—front course approaches, back course approaches, first Jim Vocell and then Pat Whitehouse in the left seat.

It came time for the last landing on Runway 23 in New Bedford. Everything was very smooth—the big radial engines strumming along on approach, flare, touchdown, and rollout. But then, as we slowed to a fast walk, the aircraft swung around hard to the left. *Ground loop!* As I was pulled away from the window by the centrifugal force, I looked out to see that we had made a 180-degree turn and were facing the approach end of the runway. The cockpit crew shut down, and we all piled out of the plane and onto the runway, which had been temporarily closed by the tower. The left tire was a little warm, but there was no damage. Nothing—no runway lights taken out.

Pat said his left knee had gotten caught under the control yoke column and he had inadvertently pressed the left brake pedal. Both pilots passed their check rides. I was brought up short, but not because Pat passed his check ride. One of the most experienced pilots around, one who flew DC-3s in the old days, had just ground looped? I wondered, what am I doing here as a novice?

On our next lesson, I felt like Luke Skywalker meeting Yoda. Dave never said anything about the incident. A good examiner considers the whole applicant: cumulative record, cognitive ability, livelihood with the airlines, volunteerism, and desire to keep the old "big round engine" birds flying as he trucked around in jet-powered airline buses while making a living. Pat Whitehouse went on to a greater reward years ago, and I feel sure he is flying heavy piston aircraft in heaven.

Like many volunteer organizations, the New England Escadrille foundered and broke down into partisan bickering and money issues. The DC-3, *Plunkett's Passion*, was sold and parted out. Parts live on in a DC-3 flying out of Titusville, Florida.

To maintain his designated examiner privileges, Dave was required to complete a check ride with the FAA every two years. He was subjected to one of his last in a Grumman Albatross amphibious aircraft on Lake Mead, Nevada. The FAA examiner sent from Washington, not type-rated in the Albatross, was nonetheless deemed best for the job. The plan was for Dave to administer a proficiency check to Chris Peatridge, acting as copilot. Dave had joint replacements and fused vertebrae, was having painful problems with his legs and back, and moved slowly.

They arrived early so Dave could be seated in the cockpit before the FAA official arrived. Dave cautioned Chris, "I'm going to put you through the wringer on this ride."

Chris thought, "Okay…I'm typed in the airplane." The FAA examiner arrived and was brought aboard the Albatross. He was introduced to Dave and strapped into the jump seat, formerly the radio operator/navigator position, directly behind the copilot.

THE OBSERVER'S SEAT IN THE ALBATROSS IS DIRECTLY BEHIND THE COPILOT'S SEAT.

From this position, the examiner could observe Dave's actions but could not see what Chris was doing with the control yoke or pedals. A cockpit voice recording of the flight might run like this:

> FAA EXAMINER. Gentlemen, I'm kinda tight on schedule. Let's get this show on the road.

> DAVE FRAWLEY. Chris, did you check those nosewheel chocks?

> CHRIS PEATRIDGE. Jeez, I'm pretty sure.

> DAVE. Pretty sure don't make it! Get your ass outa that seat, go verify, and gimme a thumbs-up if they are out.

CHRIS *unbuckles, dismounts, walks around the aircraft again, notes that the nosewheel chocks are already out, and gives Dave a thumbs-up. The FAA examiner has unbuckled and gotten out of his seat and is looking over Dave's shoulder.*

CHRIS. Captain, the chocks are out.

DAVE. Gimme the prestart checklist.

CHRIS *runs the numerous steps required before starting engines.*

CHRIS. Prestart checklist complete.

DAVE. Did you forget something?

CHRIS. Gee, I don't think so.

DAVE. Did you brief our passenger on what we are doing today and on the emergency exits?

CHRIS. Aw Jesus, Dave, I thought you guys would have talked about that.

DAVE. Brief him!

CHRIS *gets out of his seat, briefs the FAA examiner on the mission, fuel on board, shows him the hatches overhead in the cockpit, takes him back to the cabin doors that could be jettisoned in flight, then straps him tightly into the military harness in the jump seat.*

DAVE. Now, I don't wanna be telling you again. I want you to adhere to that checklist with no crap. I don't want any mistakes. It's my check ride, and I don't want you screwing it up.

CHRIS. Yes, sir. We're ready to start number two.

Following Dave's commands, Chris gets both engines running, reaching across the cockpit for the boost pump, starter, and magneto switches. Dave would have difficulty reaching these in his condition but he can reach the overhead throttles between them.

DAVE. You all set back there, Cap'n?

EXAMINER. I'm totally impressed. You guys are right on the money. I'm ready if you are.

DAVE. Now look it, I told you before, I don't want any jerking on the damn throttles. I want a smooth transition. Make sure you back me up on takeoff.

CHRIS. Yes, Captain.

It would have appeared that Chris was backing up Dave's hands on the throttles, but Chris provided the muscle, and Dave's hands followed along. The Albatross is a "heavy stick," being a thirty-thousand-pound aircraft with non-boosted controls. Chris assisted at times, unobserved in the right seat.

EXAMINER. You think we could do one water landing?

DAVE. No problem. I'll take you to a real good lake.

With Chris's assistance, they complete the required maneuvers.

EXAMINER. Are we gonna be having lunch today?

DAVE. Absolutely, if you have the time.

EXAMINER. It's about noontime now, and I have a four o'clock flight back to Washington. Let's head back to the airport.

On the turn to final approach at the airport, Dave starts mushing, getting slow. Chris has to gently push the control yoke forward and assist with the landing, all the while calling out checklist items and taking required actions in the cockpit—flaps selected down and set, landing gear down and checked, mixtures rich, props high-RPM. They taxi to the ramp.

While waiting for the idling engines to cool down, Dave pulls out the flight manual and asks Chris a "bonehead" oral exam question regarding an emergency procedure. Chris answers correctly.

DAVE. All right, it's about time you're paying attention.

They shut both engines down.

DAVE. Set the parking brake, and don't forget—you've always set it, put the friggin' chocks in, and then you leave the brake on. Don't leave the brake on this time!

CHRIS *exits the aircraft, puts the nosewheel chocks in place, then returns to the cockpit, and releases the parking brake. In the back of the Albatross, he overhears:*

EXAMINER. Jesus Christ, Dave, you're a son of a bitch.

DAVE. You gotta teach these kids the right way, and if I don't, I shouldn't be in this business.

EXAMINER. You're a great guy. This is fun; let's go to lunch.

Dave had one more check ride with the Feds before he died. That time, too, he was helped into the Albatross cockpit before the examiner arrived. Thus was the love, support, and respect brought forth for Dave Frawley, a man who devoted his entire life to training aviators—a man in failing health who still had a great deal to give and teach.

On December 13, 2005, David Frawley contacted the Mattapoisett Police Department saying he was missing four checks that he believed had been stolen, two from his checkbook and two he was expecting from an insurance settlement.[1] Three days later, at age eighty-five, he was found dead in his underwear at the bottom of the stairs in his home. His neck was broken. David had recently renewed his second-class airman's medical certificate after joint replacement.

A police patrolman observed several details that seemed out of the ordinary.[2] A lift chair at the top of the stairs was not in the proper position. Scuff marks or blood on either side of the walls would indicate a fall, but the patrolman found none. The position

David was found in at the bottom of the stairs seemed strange for a man his size. The close friend who found David clearly stated that David would never have come down the stairs in just his underwear. He stated that in the past, David would make the neighbor wait downstairs until he was able to get a robe or pants on.

Robert Moore, David's attorney and close friend, came to the residence and advised the police that it would be a good idea if they took a look at Robert's son-in-law, Michael Picewick. Robert stated he wouldn't put it past Michael to do something like this. It appeared there was something suspicious about the whole case. The police contacted the credit union regarding the missing checks. One check, a clear forgery, was made out to Michael Picewick; the other was deposited in the account of Michael's wife, Robert Moore's stepdaughter. Two checks from the auto insurance company had also been deposited into Michael's accounts.

SouthCoastToday, the local newspaper, picks up the story:

> Mr. Picewick was hired by the police in the summer of 2001, but fired in 2002. Chief Mary E. Lyons said he was dismissed after the department discovered that he'd forged and altered his paramedic certifications.
>
> Court records said that Mr. Picewick was first named as a possible suspect in the check fraud investigation by his father-in-law, Robert Moore -- Mr. Frawley's friend and lawyer. Mr. Moore also was a member of the Police Department for 14 years. "As far as I'm concerned, as far as my family is concerned, he is not a part of this family anymore," Mr. Moore said of Mr. Picewick...
>
> Mr. Frawley considered Mr. Picewick a friend, and the younger man had done work for him in the past, court records show. Mr. Moore, the executor of Mr. Frawley's estate, said he went to the police as soon as he discovered an irregularity in his client's checking. "It was a terrible shock," he said. "Nobody wants to think that someone in their family, or someone married into their family, would do that."...
>
> Although the checks were deposited into his stepdaughter's account, Mr. Moore said, she had no knowledge of any wrongdoing. "Whatever Michael did, whatever that lowlife did, my daughter did not have anything to do with it," he said. He said he hadn't

spoken to Ms. Picewick since yesterday, and did not want to speak
for her about the couple's relationship...[3]

Police arrested Michael for stealing a total of $9,590 from Frawley, and he was re-
leased on $2,500 bail. He was charged with three counts each of larceny against a per-
son over sixty-five, forgery, and passing on forged documents with intent to defraud.[4]
After "admitting to sufficient findings" to the charges, his case was "continued without
a finding." Michael was ordered to pay restitution to Dave's estate, and the case was
closed.[5]

Three years later Robert Moore was publicly reprimanded by the Massachusetts
Board of Bar Overseers for his handling of Dave Frawley's estate. Substituting their
names for the terms respondent and testator, the report reads, "Moore received a public reprimand for preparing a will for Frawley that gave Moore's wife and stepdaughters
a substantial bequest from a person to whom Moore, his wife, and his stepdaughters
were not related." Through another attorney, Dave had previously executed a will that
made no provision for Robert's wife or his three stepdaughters. In December 2007 the
conflicting wills were resolved in a compromise accepted by the court.[6]

In 2013 the Massachusetts Supreme Judicial Court recommended Robert's law license be suspended for three months but stayed this punishment based on his meeting
certain conditions. Again, the case related to a dead man's will. In this case Robert was
executor and was sanctioned for failure to probate the estate in a timely manner, failure
to distribute the estate evenly, failure to keep proper records, and charging excessive
fees.[7]

The *Boston Globe* summarized Dave's memorable career:

> Richard Porter, a friend and aviation journalist, said Dave was
> smart, sometimes abrasive, and a near-legend in the world of pi-
> lots and airplanes. "Dave was a very brilliant, crusty old man,"
> said Porter... "If he liked you, he loved you. If he didn't like you,
> you knew it."...
>
> A specialist in flying older aircraft with radial engines, Frawley
> was, at various points in his career, the only instructor in the
> world who could legally certify a new pilot in some rare types of
> aircraft. "Dave was the instructor of the instructors."[8]

It was an inglorious end for a glorious aviator, and it raised questions. Police chief
Mary Lyons wrote, "We found his death, particularly the circumstances of his death,
suspicious. The coroner ruled his death accidental. No one was charged criminally for

his death." Regarding David's demise, Chris Peatridge said, "It was quite incestuous to say the least and I don't think anybody down there wants to rake the leaves."

NEW BEDFORD TO BEDFORD

—m—

Our connection with Waco '923 is eloquently told by my friend and partner Bill Midon: He graciously agreed to contribute this chapter to the book.

IT STARTED WITH A CALL FROM MY NEW partner, John Wood, asking me if I had ever thought of a Waco biplane. I was sure it was a crank call and he was pulling my leg because, for more than a few years, I had been transfixed by the thought of flying and owning a biplane. One strike against the idea was New England weather, which would limit utility to about seven months a year. John protested that he was not pulling my leg, explaining the circumstance that resulted in the availability of a 1940 Waco close by in New Bedford, Massachusetts. My response: "John, there were only a few books published on the Waco biplanes. Three of them are sitting on my bookshelf. Yes, I am absolutely interested in considering this!"

With that, we were soon on our way to New Bedford to take a close look at this beautifully restored airplane. It didn't take long before concerns about the practicality of owning such a bird went by the wayside. New England weather? Hey—we get some nice blue-sky days in the winter! What's not to like? This beautiful bird needed someone to love it.

Buying the airplane was the easy part since we were dealing with Chris Cunningham. We were fortunate to find a machine of such provenance, built locally from scratch by the person who would maintain it during our entire ownership. Chris assured us that he thought our acquiring the airplane was a great idea.

Training began in earnest during the time prior to taking delivery. My tailwheel time was exactly zero. I spent a few hours in a Decathlon experiencing the intricacies and delights of tailwheel airplane flying. My primary flight training had been in Piper Cherokees. I thought rudder pedals were to steer the airplane on the ground and hardly ever used them in flight. The Decathlon was a great airplane for introductory tailwheel flying. You could focus on the control inputs and had a very clear view of the runway out front. That clear view would disappear once we took possession of the Waco.

My first flight in the Waco was with a remarkably experienced ex–air force, ex-airline, master aerobatic pilot. I couldn't have been in better hands. My second flight

141

was the real eye-opener. The runway had a thirty-degree crosswind, eighteen gusting to twenty-eight knots; it was not a good day for a low-time tailwheel pilot. The takeoff went fine, and twenty minutes in the air doing maneuvers was joyful. The three-point landing was another story. I did not have the fuselage straight, and the tail started to swing around. The instructor immediately called, "I've got it," barely salvaging the landing—but not before slightly scraping the left wingtip. At times, even the best hands are clearly not good enough!

He was beside himself because, as I later learned, he had never had so much as an incident throughout his air force career or his years of commercial and competition aerobatic flying. It was a humbling experience for us both. My confidence was barely salvaged by his insistence that it was his fault and we shouldn't have been flying. My takeaway, influenced by additional hours of flying, was that wheel landings, two-point with the tail still flying, were much more palatable on tarmac. The big, fat rubber tires really stick when they touch down on asphalt. The airplane's fuselage has to be straight. If it is the least bit angled from the centerline, the Waco will tell you immediately to press hard on a rudder pedal to correct. Speed control is the other factor, and being too fast only makes things more difficult. Three-point landings are for grass airfields, which have "give," allowing the tires to slide a bit to make up for less-than-perfect piloting technique.

Chris Cunningham made the wingtip repair in short order, and the airplane was none the worse for wear. I gained a deeper respect for just how quickly a tailwheel airplane can get out of control. I flew a turboprop for ten years, I've flown a twin-engine jet for nine years now, and I've piloted a helicopter for fifteen years. None of these birds have ever commanded my absolute, unequivocal attention during landing as the Waco did…in any wind!

My first real adventure soon followed. I approached my friend John and asked him what he thought of the idea of bringing the airplane to Florida for the winter: "Do you think that you would take advantage of it being in Venice?" He assured me he would, and having the Waco there would be the best motivation in the world to make Florida a regular stop during the long, cold New England winter. Given my limited hours in the Waco, I connected with Paul, a summer air-tour pilot at Martha's Vineyard's Katama Airpark, the largest grass airport in the United States. Paul was on board, as he migrated to Florida every fall.

On one of the last days of October 2005, we departed. The morning was cold and brisk, but clear, blue-sky weather. Winds were also cooperative, and at five hundred feet above the beach, we averaged a ground speed of eighty miles per hour or so from the tip of New Jersey to Florida. The weather over the entire East Coast for the following few days was going to be fine, supporting the compelling logic of heading south for the winter. It also presented a wonderful opportunity for two days of training. Paul did his best to impart all the knowledge he could over the drone of the engine.

To say we packed lightly is an understatement. The baggage compartment in the Waco is only slightly larger than an automobile glove box, and that is where you carry cans of engine oil. We flew four two-hour legs that day, arriving in Ocracoke late in the afternoon. We stayed at the local pub/hotel, and I went to bed with the sound of the engine still droning in my ears.

The next day we awoke to clear, beautiful weather for the final day of our trip. The flights were uneventful but slow. We followed the intercoastal waterway all the way down, and it was amazing to see the parade of boats, lined up one after another, heading south for the winter. At one point we were at five hundred feet over the intercoastal, passing immediately over a beautiful sailboat. We waved at the sailors, and they enthusiastically waved back. Five minutes later I looked back to see the same sailboat. They were motoring, but nonetheless, it confirmed our slow ground speed. I realized then that I might miss my commercial flight home. We stopped at Orlando, and Paul pressed on to Venice.

Recently, I discovered that I have some minor hearing loss. I don't doubt that that trip contributed to it. However, I wouldn't trade the experience for anything. The bird's eye view of the East Coast, from the beautiful beaches of the New Jersey Southern Shore to Kitty Hawk, North Carolina, to the Lowcountry in South Carolina was unforgettable. It was truly special and one of those "I'm so glad I did it in retrospect" adventures.

The pilot in Florida called Chris Cunningham to ask, "What's the paint code for the Waco?"

I asked, "Why would you need the paint code?"

"Well, somebody brushed up against it just slightly with a car," the pilot said. As the conversation continued, his story kept changing until the truth finally came out: turns out he'd let another pilot fly from the front cockpit, and that pilot had looked down at something during the landing rollout. He'd felt the Waco swing and looked up in time to ride along in the ground loop. One of the aluminum wheel halves was busted, they'd dragged a wingtip, and the shop had to double up the aft spar, and repair two ribs. We asked Chris to fly to Spruce Creek and inspect the work while the mechanic had the airplane apart.

Hampton Airfield, in southern New Hampshire, is one of those classic grass strips with open-shed T-hangars and a WWII-vintage building housing a restaurant and modest flight school, adorned by a sofa that I think my mother gave to the Salvation Army in the late sixties. Hampton is just a thirty-minute flight up the coast from our home base, Hanscom Field, and with its wonderful on-field restaurant and forgiving grass runway, it was a frequent "$100 hamburger" destination. I have numerous memories or flying into Hampton—most good, one scary, one sad.

One beautiful late summer afternoon, I took a friend up to Hampton. We could walk to a nearby sandwich shop, get dinner, and enjoy watching various vintage aircraft take off and land. When we arrived on this particular evening, I was surprised to be greeted by a fellow with two red batons who was enthusiastically ushering us over to a parking spot. With the engine shut down, we climbed out of the airplane and were met with a hearty "Welcome to Pete and Kate's wedding rehearsal party!"

Had we been better dressed, we may have pretended we were invited guests. In wrinkled shorts and T-shirts, we admitted that we were just flying in for an evening's respite and knew nothing about the rehearsal dinner that was in full swing. We enjoyed our sandwiches with the music from the live band in the background. Summer evening flights in the Waco were always a highlight, and watching the sunset from the open cockpit never got old.

All pilots practice soft-field takeoffs and landings. I don't recall specifically practicing soft-field taxiing, though I do recall the one rule if the ground is soft: keep the airplane rolling.

I flew into Hampton one early spring morning. It was blue sky and, though still quite cold, was going to warm up during the day. I landed on the hard turf, taxied to the parking spot, and enjoyed a nice breakfast.

When I left, the ground was considerably softer, as the sun had warmed things up nicely. While taxiing out for departure, I made a tight turn onto the runway, stepped on the left brake—and the airplane came to an abrupt halt. It would not budge from that spot—at about a right angle to the runway. I shut down, got out, and saw that my left tire was dug deeply into the soft, thawed mud. A fellow driving by in a pickup truck observed my dilemma and offered to help. We lifted the Waco's tail and aligned the airplane down the runway. I jumped in, buckled up, started the engine, and was off in a whiz, none the worse for wear.

My scary memory of Hampton visits came on a beautiful summer Saturday: as I flew downwind for a landing to the south, I suddenly experienced a windscreen full of airplane—a motorized glider, to be exact. He had no radio or did not use it. I made a very steep turn to get clear. That was as close as I ever wanted to be to a midair collision. It really brought forth just how restricted the visibility is in a biplane, with its wings and struts and wires. That day I learned that you can't be too careful—or too lucky!

My sad moment came unexpectedly on another Saturday morning. As partners, John and I share a helicopter as well as the biplane. That morning, we arrived at the hangar having unexpectedly double-booked the Waco. He was there with our former hangar-mate and fellow aviator Avi, an accomplished radiologist with a humble, quiet demeanor. The double-booking had a ready solution. I agreed that I would fly the Waco to Hampton. John would take Avi in the helicopter. After breakfast, we would switch aircraft. That way, Avi would be able to enjoy time in each machine.

We found a table at the always-busy Airfield Café. I asked Avi, "How's everything going? I haven't seen you in months."

Avi hesitated and then, in a hoarse voice interrupted by frequent coughing, said, "I've been better." That caught my attention. He then said, "I've been diagnosed with Stage IV lung cancer." You could have knocked me off my chair with a feather. Here I was, about to enjoy the camaraderie of my fellow aviators, only to find out that one may soon ascend to the ultimate flight level.

I had no idea what to say. I still don't. Avi passed away less than six months later, leaving behind a wife and two young sons. I flew back home in the helicopter, despite the film of water over my eyes restricting visibility. Avi's memorial service was held in a big aircraft hangar, and the Waco was front and center.

A dear friend of mine invited me to Martha's Vineyard one weekend. Two of their young adult children would be visiting and would dearly love to have a ride in the biplane. They had rented a house in Edgartown, only a few minutes' ride from Katama Airfield. The Waco loved flying there, likely because two of its kin, both vintage UPF-7s, were based there. I enjoyed a couple of hours sharing the beauty of open-cockpit flight as we danced S-turns over the Vineyard shoreline, gawking at beachgoers—who were likely gawking back at us. Waves from the biplane's crew were always enthusiastically met with hearty waves from those on the ground.

WACO '923 OVER NEW ENGLAND.

Having briefed the weather earlier in the day, I knew that a front was approaching from the south and that the weather would turn sour later. The forecast suggested that leaving by midafternoon would keep me in visual conditions. We finished the rides early, and the sky was still blue overhead. I was impressed with how perfectly I was executing my plan. The blue, hazy sky above was certainly darkening well to the south, just as forecast. I took off for my return flight to Bedford. As I passed through seven hundred feet or so, mindful of the controlled airspace around the Martha's Vineyard airport, I suddenly went into the clouds.

With no attitude indicator, my first thought was to hold the stick absolutely steady. I realized I had to make a quick decision—continue to climb or immediately descend—and just as I went to gently push the stick forward to descend, I popped out of a two-hundred-foot layer back into visual conditions on top of the cloud deck. The Waco has a turn and bank indicator similar to the one used by Charles Lindbergh to fly the North Atlantic in instrument conditions. I am more impressed than ever by his feat after that flight. The rest of my flight home was in the clear.

I always enjoyed flying the Waco to community fly-ins. The airplane attracted a lot of attention from the crowds, not all of it good. I recall one morning at the airport in Mansfield, Massachusetts. I taxied to parking, shut the engine down, got out of the airplane, and walked over to a couple of the organizers to thank them. We were engaging in pleasantries when I turned to look back at the airplane to see a swarm of children ready to climb on the wing. I didn't want to scare anyone, but I immediately ran to the airplane and explained that the wings were covered by fabric, which could be easily perforated. Disaster was averted, but it was closer than I would have preferred.

It's fascinating to observe experiences with different children. Many are cautious, but others seem to have no reservations—"feral children," as my other airplane partner once noted. After that experience I laminated signs in bold print that implored "PLEASE DO NOT TOUCH." I also realized that day that my enjoyment of a community fly-in is limited to a twenty-foot radius around the airplane. I carried a roll of duct tape with me from that day on. At least that would get me home in a worst-case scenario!

Both my partner John and I have beautiful, classic hard shell leather helmets manufactured by Campbell Aero Classics in New Zealand. Campbell's website says they recreate yesteryear's golden era of aviation, allowing the pilot to relive the adventure, exhilaration, passion, fun, and romance of flying—I was definitely signing up for that!

I always flew with that helmet. The noise attenuation was passive but better than anything else I tried. The authenticity of the look was undeniable. At one community fly-in, I took the helmet out of the cockpit and offered it to an onlooker so that she could have her picture taken while wearing the helmet and standing in front of the Waco. Within minutes a line formed of people wanting to wear the helmet while posing for a photo session with the airplane. It was apparent that the helmet was of at least as much interest as the airplane. There's no telling how many Christmas photographs featured that leather helmet with the Waco in the background.

I would be remiss not to compliment the tower personnel at our home base, Hanscom Field. As the major reliever airport for Boston's Logan Airport, every day the field supports numerous corporate jet operations, charter airliners for sports teams, and air force test aircraft. In my twelve years of flying the Waco in and out of Bedford, the tower personnel handled our seventy-mile-per-hour departures and arrivals with aplomb, mixing us in with the much faster "big iron."

I headed home one afternoon knowing that we were in for building thunderstorms. I was on a long straight-in approach to the runway when the tower advised that there was a fast Learjet behind me. The calm female voice then issued what I knew to be the right instruction: "Waco '923, make a 360-degree turn to the south to allow the Learjet to land. Caution—wake turbulence. Oh, and caution, there's Level 5 rain activity to the south."

The massive, dark rain cloud was clearly visible as I made a tight turn. As I rejoined the final approach, above the Learjet's final descent path, the rain started. No problem. The slipstream kept the rain over the windscreen and out of the cockpit. All was good as I touched down. In fact, with a bit of rain on the runway reducing the typical stickiness of the tires on the tarmac, I made a smooth landing. Immediately, I realized that my friend, the slipstream, was gone. As I taxied, water started pouring into the cockpit, augmented by the vast surface area of the upper wing. And then I remembered: stopping in front of our hangar would bring the ultimate outdoor cleansing followed by the incredibly slow pull into the hangar.

John and I have had a few conversations around the question, "Is it time to sell the Waco?" The constraints of the New England winters had us flying the Waco for a limited number of hours during the typical April-to-October season. We had had a great run with the airplane, but logic suggested that it may be time for someone else to become the custodian of this wonderful old bird. I sensed that I should take advantage of every opportunity to fly the Waco a few more times.

The only FAA-approved ice runway in the Lower 48 is Alton Bay (B18), located on Lake Winnipesaukee, New Hampshire. Volunteers require the ice to be at least one foot thick to support aircraft, cars, and trucks, and the airport is usually open four to six weeks per year.

We have flown a helicopter to Alton Bay numerous times, but the stars aligned to make landing the biplane on the ice runway the ultimate flying experience. The community's winter carnival was underway. It was a remarkably warm February day with light winds. Nonetheless, I was acutely aware of proper control technique. The last thing any pilot wants to be remembered for is losing directional control of an airplane while landing in front of a crowd. Speed control was right on, and the landing was

BILL MIDON REFUELS THE WACO AFTER LANDING ON IHE ICE RUNWAY AT ALTON BAY.

without incident Taxiing to the parking spot with people milling all around really held my attention. With the big radial engine blocking the view, I was completely reliant on the wing walkers.

After a wonderful breakfast at the nearby café, we set out to return to Bedford. Again, the taxi out to the ice runway was precarious and worrisome, given the people strolling about. I felt a tremendous sense of relief once the airplane was airborne! The arrival back at Hanscom was on one hand uneventful. However, when I was bringing the tug out to tow the airplane back to the hangar, I witnessed the most incredible sky I have ever seen.

—Bill Midon[*]

---

[*] Bill is a father of four, proud grandfather, and an entrepreneur in technology and real estate development. He has been flying for forty-plus years.

A FAMILY AFFAIR

—m—

Acquiring Waco '923 was a dream come true and allowed me to share this dream with family and friends.

ON MY TRIPS TO NEW BEDFORD IN 1997 to fly the DC-3 with Dave Frawley, I would admire Waco '923 in the hangar. It was a jewel, but I never saw it outside flying. Word had it the plane was for sale, at an asking price of two hundred grand plus. That meant it wasn't really for sale, but Dave was hanging onto this reminder of his youth as a World War II instructor. Time passed and Dave had a couple of vertebrae fused---he couldn't climb into the Waco cockpit anymore.

I've always regarded tailwheel flying as the highest form of the art. Actually, the very apex belongs to naval aviators of World War II in Grumman Wildcats, who performed non-catapult takeoffs, followed by arrested landings on small escort aircraft carriers, after strafing Japanese caves on Iwo Jima. A friend had an uncle who did that. There is good reason they are called the greatest generation.

My flying has been far more mundane. Twenty years after the greatest generation launched and recovered, I was working in Dallas as a summer engineer before heading to graduate school. There were two options available for flight instruction, the more expensive being an all-metal nosewheel Cessna 150 flown off a paved runway. For less money I chose a fabric-covered tailwheel aircraft flown off grass. I've always felt lucky that my first thirty flight hours were in a Piper Super Cub.

But as the years rolled by, I didn't do much tailwheel flying. The opportunity to combine that with the lure of the open cockpit in an aviation classic was too much, and I was excited that Bill Midon got on board too. I had gotten to know Dave Frawley and he encouraged us to make an offer. We bought the UPF-7 for $137,500. After a few hours of training with a qualified instructor, I started taking people for biplane rides. Daughter Diana describes her experience:

> The first, and sadly only, time I went up in the Waco was a late summer morning my second year in business school. I was worried about my career. The world was slowly coming apart due to

151

the global financial crisis, and I wondered if any of the jobs I had interviewed for would come through. When my dad suggested going up in the Waco that morning, I was eager to join. I was in an aviation state of mind.

It was early, and I was a tired. As we pulled up to Hanscom Field, I chugged the rest of my coffee and hopped out to put on one of his Nomex flight suits. I helped him guide the plane out the hangar and was surprised by how light it felt. It was a bluebird day and the sun shone brightly on the hunter green wings. There was a seat in the front near the engine and one just behind. I followed Dad's instructions, climbing up the walkway on the left wing. I was reaching for the rear seat when he said, "No, you are sitting up front. I am in the back." I knew the Waco was a training plane but forgot I would be up front on my own.

The seat leather was worn, and I was surprised how wide it was for just one person. My dad helped to fasten the old seat belt and climbed in back. As he was putting his shoulder harness on, I pulled the mic up to my mouth, "Do we have parachutes? This seatbelt is really loose, and the seat is huge. I could slide across it. Where are the parachutes?" "We don't need parachutes," he replied, "We aren't going to do any aerobatics and it will be a smooth flight." My heart skipped a beat. I trusted my dad implicitly but looking around at this single engine plane, I was aware that there would be no Plan B in the air.

I know a part of my dad grimaced when I asked questions like that. Most likely because he knew I was a little scared and simply lacked his passion. He probably frowned when he looked at the back of my head to see me crossing myself on takeoff. The truth was, I started doing that as a young girl because I watched my grandmother do it. She would cross herself every time she flew, and I just started copying it. It didn't mean I didn't trust him, it just reminded me of her. I knew there was never a chance I would be in danger when I flew with my father. In fact, I felt safer in the air with him than with anyone else.

"Clear!" I heard my dad holler. The propeller flicked around a couple of times and the engine started with a sputter, a cloud of blue smoke and the smell of oil and gasoline. It ran ragged for a little bit, then I heard the familiar purring sound of a flying machine. My dad banged my knees swinging his control stick back-and-forth and started taxiing towards the runway. We turned from one side to the other as I watched the hangars and building facilities pass by. "Isn't it a beautiful day?" my dad said. It *was* a beautiful day. This would be a great ride.

Dad taxied the Waco up to the runway threshold, stopped and ran the engine up to full power. The propwash swirled around the cockpit. I could I hear him talking to the tower, and finally he asked, "Diana, are you ready?" "Uh, yup!" We taxied out, I saw my throttle lever move forward, and we started gaining speed. Then all of a sudden, we took flight. The ground pulled away; houses, cars and roads began to shrink, as objects became part of a make-believe world. The sun was so bright on the wings, and it was such a smooth ascent.

As we leveled off, I became acutely aware of two things. First, we were in a convertible going a thousand miles an hour, just out there in the elements. How in the world had pilots trained in this thing in the middle of winter? On the ground I had felt a little warm in the flight suit, but now the air was cooler, and it was nice to have on. I was scared of heights, but this fear was somehow never triggered on the airlines or my father's other planes. Perhaps because in those, you had a roof over your head, and you couldn't stick your arm out of a nonexistent window. Either way, in my mind I started to panic.

No sooner had the anxiety set in, did I hear a voice over the headset. "Diana, can you hear me?" Dad's southern drawl buried under years in Yankee land, was still there. It came out when he was enjoying himself and he was the happiest in the air. "Yes! Yes, I hear you?" I nervously yelled back over the wind. "Do you see the control stick in front of you? Take hold of it." "Okay, I have it."

"Alright Diana, learning is all about application. The plane is yours." "What? What do you mean it's *MINE*?" I nervously yelled back. "It means you are flying. Now let's do some of this together. Right now, you are in level flight. We are flying at three thousand feet and going 85 miles an hour. Do you see the altimeter? It reads like a clock. Do you see how fast we are going?" Jesus. "Um yes, I see 85."

"Good. Now let's get a feel for the controls a bit. Try to do a little turn," Dad instructed. "No! No! What do you mean? I don't want to turn. Let's just stay straight." "Okay that's fine. We can go straight for a while. Just keep it level. You are doing a great job. Look outside at how much horizon is over the wing on each side, that's how you keep it level."

At first, I held the stick tight in both hands and kept it as still as I possibly could. A wave of nerves rushed over me. I was absolutely terrified, but I didn't have time to process the fear. I blocked everything out, re-gripped the stick and focused on making slight adjustments to stay level with the horizon.

Dad's voice came through the headset again, "That's good. You have a nice touch. Okay, now we need to keep an eye out for traffic." My dad had been talking back and forth on the radio and I had simply tuned it out. There was a Cessna coming up on our right side. I picked my head up and scanned the skies. "I don't see it," I yelled. "Hold what you've got and take another look, he said." I looked around again and saw the other plane drifting below us. "I see it. I see it!" He reminded me that we need to keep track of who is up here with us. Especially in a plane with wings blocking the view. The tower is there to help but as the pilot, you always have to be aware.

"Okay, now let's do a small bank to the left." "Really?" I replied. "Yes, you can do it. Gently move the stick towards the left." If I had the courage to close my eyes, I would have but instead I ever so slightly angled to the left. "That's good. Nice turn, Diana. Now let's roll level again and then try the other side. Take a minute and then start turning towards the right." I slowly got the plane straight again and started to bank to the right. "Good, that's very good."

By now, I was gripping the control column so tightly that my hands were starting to hurt. My knuckles were white, and my palms were sweating. But I was flying. On my own. The wind was rushing past us like a freight train, the engine was drowning out any other sound except for my father's voice and the Earth was passing effortlessly by us below. Time seemed to stand still.

We had several more minutes of smooth maneuvering before Mother Earth began to wake up. It was nearing 9:30AM and the ground was starting to heat up, creating pockets of turbulence--just enough bumps to jolt me during my timid turns. "Whoa, Dad what was that? Is that some weather?" "No, we have clear skies ahead. It is just a few bumps." "Okay, well I'm scared, can you take over now?" Sure, let's start heading back." My dad took over and I finally let go. My hands were throbbing, and my heart was pounding. I had sweat dripping down the back, soaking the inside of the flight suit. But it was such an incredible rush of excitement.

As we bumped along, I looked up at the upper wing and closed my eyes. I let my mind wander. I was reminded of a movie I used to see as a child. My parents would take us to Washington, DC to visit the national museums. At the National Air and Space Museum we always made time for an IMAX showing of, *To Fly*. It began with a vignette on the history of flight and then told the story of a young wing walker. Dressed in a clown costume, he would perform at air shows. Then one day, his mentor died in a flight accident and he took over. It was sad but beautiful. Looking up at the wings of the Waco, I could only imagine the courage it took to walk them, what fortitude a person must have and what passion. And how much someone had to love, to fly.

I came back from my daydreams in the midst of landing. The plane was still jostling a bit, with that kind of machine, you felt every gust. But my father carefully guided the Waco down to kiss the ground. The wheels squeaked on the runway, we bounced

once and then taxied back towards flight operations. I unzipped
my flight suit to let some fresh air in and noticed that my stom-
ach felt a bit queasy. I reached up and carefully ran my hands
along the inside of the cockpit. It's hard to believe that just a few
lengths of steel tubing, wood strips and canvas kept us safe as we
soared.

The plane came to a stop in front of the T-hangars and all of a
sudden, I realized my breakfast was coming up. I jumped out,
ran to the edge of the grass and got sick. I crumpled down on
the asphalt as my dad quickly walked up. "Diana, that is just low-
grade fear. I got sick on my first light-plane ride, but not after
that. You did a great job and have an excellent touch." I took a
deep breath and looked up at him. "It was kind of bumpy on the
way in. I think I was just air sick." "That's okay," he reassured
me.

I got up and helped my dad put the Waco to bed. Then we
closed the hangar and drove home together. The whole way he
kept talking about the flight---how much fun it was and what
a great job I had done. When we got to the house, he walked
straight to his office and filled out my logbook, the same one I
have had since I was five years old. The entry read "Waco intro:
straight & level, turns, climb & glide." And I never felt closer to
my father or understood him more.

Daughter Jenny has her own thoughts about Waco '923:

I can close my eyes and picture the first time I flew in my dad's
biplane fifteen years ago. Being up in the air, thousands of feet
above the ground in a machine made of wood, metal and fabric was absolutely exhilarating and a bit terrifying at the same
time. However, the more times I rode in that aircraft, the more I
began to appreciate his love for it. It is a true specimen, a beautiful eighty-year-old biplane with years of history and tales to be
told. And I'm so glad that my dad has finally written down these
stories.

As I've grown over the years, I've come to appreciate his love of flying more and more and I realize how incredibly lucky I am to have flown in one of his favorite aircraft, the Waco UPF-7. My only regret is that my children did not get to experience it, but who knows, over time, maybe they will develop the same passion my dad has for flying and I will be able to continue to fly, just like a bird.

DAUGHTER DIANA STRAPPED INTO WACO '923, BEDFORD, MASSACHUSETTS.

Were there issues with the Waco? Sure, it's a flying machine, and an early one at that. I never considered it a very crashworthy aircraft. You have forty-eight gallons of highly flammable aviation gasoline just above your head in two aluminum tanks in the center section of the upper wing. Stan Parker was lucky that so little gas got loose in his wreck and then did not ignite.

I wore a fire-resistant Nomex military-surplus flying suit in the Waco---not because it was cool, but it made me feel safer and cleaner. Adding oil, fuel and servicing the tires was a dirty job, and the flying suit did not seem to mind the grime. This kept my street clothes clean, and I kept a collection of different sizes for my passengers.

The aircraft was originally delivered with two military-style bucket seats, provision for seat-pack parachutes and four-point harness restraints. In 1945 Waco '923 was converted to a crop duster by removing the front seat and replacing it with a chemical hopper. As the aircraft was converted back to carrying passengers, an "improvement" was made. Instead of the original bucket seat, a wide bench seat was installed, allowing two passengers to be carried in front. This is what made the UPF-7 so popular among scenic air tour operators.

However, it did so at the price of passenger safety. Waco '923 had one long automotive-type seat belt with two shoulder straps. A single passenger could slide left-to-right on the bench seat, and two passengers had only one shoulder harness apiece. I wished our aircraft still had the same bucket seat that I enjoyed in the rear cockpit. I wanted to take our nine-year-old grandson flying in the Waco, but considering his size, I could not figure out how strap him in securely.

My wife, Mary Kay, was not impressed by the Waco. "It's noisy, smelly and I can't see much out of the front seat. It's kind of like an aerial motorcycle." (Which is the whole idea, of course.) "It's back to World War Two and it should be in a museum." I guess she has gotten spoiled by other aircraft we have flown---they whisk you from A to B in pressurized shirt-sleeve comfort.

She *did* enjoy open cockpit flying, long ago, when we first met. That plane, a de Haviland Tiger Moth, was far more primitive. It had no electrical system and had to be propped by hand with the tail tied down. I would get her strapped in, pull the engine through to prime it, turn on the magnetos, set the throttle, and ask her not to touch anything until I got the plane started, untied, and strapped in myself. Well... that was back when, in 1973.

Why did Bill and I sell Waco '923? There were several factors. As flying goes, this aircraft is more of an end than a means. You aren't going anywhere very fast, ideally on warm days with light winds. Eventually I had taken most everyone that wanted the open cockpit experience for at least one flight. I took solo flights to maintain currency, but still our annual utilization was low. It was hard to maintain tailwheel skills while flying so few hours per year, and Bill and I were current in two other aircraft. I did fly the

Waco a few times with snow on the ground, in a surplus insulated flying suit. I found that you could lower the pilot's seat to the bottom stop to get out of the slipstream, but eventually you had to bring it back up to land. It sure felt good to get out of the cockpit and get the blood flowing afterwards.

Chris Cunningham's restoration of the Waco was marvelous, but that was nearly twenty-five years ago. More recently, Continental had recommended that their engines be overhauled every twelve years, whether or not they have reached their allotted running time. Our engine had been overhauled before an original design deficiency was cured by replacing the rear ball bearing on the crankshaft with a roller bearing. This reduced the tendency for the engine to "make metal" if the old bearing failed. According to the nameplate, Waco '923's engine went into service six months before I did, May 1943, and sooner or later it would need another overhaul, and the new rear bearing.

Similarly, the aircraft's fabric covering was approaching a quarter century in age. In principle, the fabric will last a very long time as the aircraft lived most of its life in a hangar, out of the sun's ultraviolet rays. Even then, the doped fabric dries out, develops fine cracks in places, and the plane will eventually need to be recovered. We had replaced the Waco's obsolete communication and navigation equipment with modern avionics, but sooner or later the plane would be due for overhaul.

All-in-all, Bill and I had a good run. We enjoyed flying this ancient beast, had maintained it well, and not torn it up. It was time to let someone else have their turn.

A BROKEN HEART

—m—

Behind the times in aviation technology, Waco goes out of business after the war.
A fan base springs to action to provide parts and keep the classic design alive.

In the 1930s the Waco Aircraft Company was the largest manufacturer of private aircraft in the United States. During the life of the company it delivered over four thousand planes. Its motto was Ask Any Pilot. The company was founded shortly after World War I by pilots who first started rebuilding military surplus aircraft and then developed their own designs. George "Buck" Weaver was the namesake for the Weaver Aircraft Company of Ohio. The company produced a variety of open-cockpit and enclosed-cabin biplanes and survived the Great Depression by producing sought-after designs.

As the Second World War loomed, the air forces of Brazil, Venezuela, Guatemala, and Cuba purchased Waco biplanes as trainers. The UPF-7 was evaluated by the United States as the standard military trainer but was not selected. That honor went to the Stearman Model 75, of which more than ten thousand were produced. The Stearman had interchangeable parts and was built using standardized tooling. The Waco was built more like a homebuilt aircraft, each one a little different. Sheet metal was fitted to individual aircraft, not match drilled on a fixture. Waco ramped up production to fill the UPF-7 order for civilian pilot training, finishing three aircraft per day.

Next Waco developed "...the most widely used U.S. troop/cargo glider of World War II. Constructed of fabric-covered wood and metal, the CG-4A was crewed by a pilot and copilot. It could carry thirteen troops and their equipment or a jeep; a quarter-ton truck; or a 75 mm howitzer loaded through the upward-hinged nose section. Flight testing began in 1942, and the CG-4A first went into operation in July 1943 during the Allied invasion of Sicily. It also participated in the D-Day assault on France on June 6,

1944, and in other important airborne operations in Europe and in the China-Burma-India Theater. Until late in the war, gliders were generally considered expendable in combat and were abandoned or destroyed after landing."[1]

Twelve thousand assault gliders were built, one thousand at the Waco factory.

WACO CG-4A HADRIAN ASSAULT GLIDER.

Dinosaurs are revered by adults and children everywhere, in part because they were in a class all their own before becoming extinct. Waco Aircraft Company was like an aviation dinosaur that never really caught up with the evolution of twentieth-century aircraft technology. At the end of World War II, aircraft manufacturers anticipated a boom in civilian aircraft demand from returning military pilots. They developed sleek, all-metal traveling machines such as the Beechcraft Bonanza, which would comfortably whisk a family of four along at over 150 miles per hour. Waco developed an all-metal aircraft of unconventional design. The demand did not materialize, and only a single prototype was built.

Waco was in difficult shape because it was mainly making "rag and tube" airplanes with wooden wings and steel-tubing fuselages, covered with fabric. Their philosophy seemed to be "If it was good enough for my pa, it is good enough for me." Lacking a modern product line, the company stopped building aircraft and began producing bread truck bodies, sun lamps, and log splitters. Waco closed the shop in 1965, and the company's drawings and other records were donated to the Smithsonian Institution.[2]

Airplanes are complex machines requiring periodic inspection, maintenance, and replacement of parts. How do you keep your UPF-7 flying when the last one was built in 1942 and the factory stopped building aircraft in 1946? Carefully, as the expression goes. Not surprisingly, you will have lots of help. Of the nearly 600 Waco UPF-7s built, about 180 are still listed in the FAA registry. Some are flying, some are being rebuilt, and some are in pieces on the hangar floor.

Who are the tribal elders, high priests, keepers of the flame in the Waco world? There are two so-called "type clubs," as in aircraft type, dedicated to the aircraft. From its website we learn about the earliest:

> The National Waco Club was founded in 1958 by a small group of six Waco enthusiasts who felt that they should have an organization to support their hobby and love of owning and flying Waco airplanes...
>
> Ray Brandly was a B-17 pilot who had come home to Dayton, Ohio after WWII and resumed flying after a 10-year hiatus. Ray became interested in Waco airplanes when he and several others got together and purchased a 1941 Waco UPF-7 in the mid-fifties. Ray was so smitten with Wacos that he soon purchased several more. The Waco Aircraft Company in Troy, Ohio was still in business, although they were no longer building aircraft. Ray quickly became acquainted with President Clayton Bruckner and a lifetime friendship evolved.
>
> Waco had always maintained that no Waco airplane would ever want for a spare or replacement part. Consequently, there existed a large inventory of new parts for practically every model of Waco airplane that had been built...In...1957, Mr. Bruckner approved the sale of these parts to Ray Brandly, never suspecting a movement would soon be underway to restore the many

forgotten and sadly neglected Waco airplanes that were still a common sight at many airports around the country.

...After a sunny day of flying and great camaraderie with the other antique airplane enthusiasts, the Waco owners got together and decided to form a club. Since Ray was the go-to man for Waco parts, he naturally was chosen to lead the club. Ray and the others went home and soon Ray was receiving letters and phone calls from other Waco owners across the country, simply by word of mouth. It was soon decided that the club needed a newsletter and Ray took on that responsibility as well...

...In 1959, the National Waco Club [hosted] its first fly-in gathering at the new South Dayton Airport...The first gathering was a grand event with approximately 10 Wacos attending...By the late 1980's [there] routinely [were] close to 40 Wacos attending every gathering.

...The National Waco Club Fly-in [was moved] to Wynkoop Airport in Mt. Vernon, Ohio in 1989. Wynkoop Airport is a beautiful, all-grass airport that has been run by the Wynkoop family since the late 1940's. Owner Brian Wynkoop was more than happy to offer his airport to the National Waco Club and a friendship with the Club evolved and still continues to this day...

Since that time, many things have changed...The newsletter went from four pages to twelve, mailed bi-monthly. Every National Reunion now has a free early-bird cookout and a free Corn Boil for all attending members. Participation awards are given to every pilot flying a Waco to the Reunion. A fund-raiser auction is held every year at the Reunion following the banquet. [There are] owner-operator forums...on such topics as restoration, aircraft coverings...[and] engine overhauls...The Club also maintains the largest collection of Waco photos in the U.S., as well as a huge collection of manuals and brochures.[3]

Forrest Lovley has a tale to tell. The Waco F2, built 1931–32, has the same engine and wing area as the UPF-7 but is five hundred to seven hundred pounds lighter and thus has much better performance. Forrest had the parts for a number of these and began rebuilding them in Minnesota:

> In the late eighties and early nineties, the F2 went from being a $30,000 valuable antique to a $130,000 valuable antique practically overnight. So it paid to resurrect old parts; I was in that business and built up a few of them. Ray Brandly founded and ran the club, and I give him credit for that. But he was getting old and slipping. He was thinking in fifties and sixties dollars and was of the opinion that anytime a Waco, especially an F2, sold for more than $30,000, there had to be drugs and illegal money involved.

> Brandly and a friend got to gossiping with each other and expanded on their stories with each other until they believed unbelievable things. They called the FBI and said, "There is this guy up in Minnesota that is building up airplanes from scratch, and he's putting long-range tanks in them. The tanks are not for fuel; that's where they're going to hide the drugs. The guy's wife works in a bank, and she launders the money for him."

> I had a guy building wings for me, and I was welding up fuselages and landing gear. One day the FBI dropped in to see us and proceeded with their investigation, which turned out to be nothing. It's really scary when the FBI interviews you and tells you that you are a "person of interest." It was hard on my wife because she *did* work in a bank.

> You can't blame the FBI because it had all the stuff they are trained to look for—drugs, laundering money, and a tipster. It was a big deal for a while, but the FBI found out they had been had and went on their way. Ray Brandly denied it all, denied as he was walking away because he knew he had been caught. There are F2s all over the country that I've resurrected, and I'm not done—I've got a couple left. In that era, they went from $30,000 to $130,000 to $330,000, and now they are back down to $200,000 apiece.

I filed a Freedom of Information Act request in order to find out
what they did and what the file contained, and still to this day I
cannot get access to it. The FBI does not have to release any files
for cases that are still active. Being as they knew they had been
had, they didn't want their face to ever be rubbed into it, so once
a year somebody opens the file, looks at it, closes it again, and
that classifies it as an open investigation.

Brandly bought out the parts from the Waco factory, tractor
trailer-loads, and he sold them off for years. He'd sell a wing for
only two hundred bucks. Brandly did a lot of good things…but
he went out on a bad note. At fly-ins he would not let a modern
Waco park next to the others—it was counterfeit.

Another owner said Brandly wanted you to have original 1930s-vintage Waco air
in your tires to park with the others at a reunion. Stearmans or newly produced Wacos
need not apply. People at an airport in Hamilton, Ohio, said they could not deal with
him in setting up a fly-in, and that is how the American WACO* Club got started twenty
years ago.[4]

The rift does not rank with the Protestant Reformation, but a separate Waco type
club was created. Its annual reunion is held at the Creve Coeur airport, near Saint
Louis. Many Waco owners and enthusiasts are members of both clubs, and they provide
untold benefits. Staffed by volunteers, they are fantastic venues for sharing technical
knowledge, obtaining parts, participating in flight training, acquiring insurance, buying and selling aircraft, and establishing lifelong friendships.

The club reunions are grand gatherings of the clan. Beautifully restored aircraft
are everywhere, arrayed on the manicured grass of the Mount Vernon airport. A steady
stream of aircraft make low passes, radial engines rumbling pleasantly, as a corn boil
lunch is held under a shady grove of trees alongside the 3,300-foot grass runway. A table
offers bumper stickers: "Real Pilots Fly Round Engines" and "Radial Engines Don't Leak
Oil, They Are Just Marking Their Territory." Experts conduct seminars on the care and
feeding of your round engine and the latest restoration techniques. Old-timers tell tales
of aircraft being damaged during the last year, but others have just finished multiyear
restorations. Young people are inculcated to the ways of the Waco.

The Historic Aircraft Restoration Museum at Creve Coeur houses the biggest gathering of Wacos in the world, not to mention a vast collection of other airworthy antique
aircraft. Walking along the hangars is a flying buff's dream—a Waco in this one, a

---

* This club capitalizes the company acronym; the other does not.

Corsair in the next. At a recent gathering I spotted a sibling of Waco '923, only three tail numbers higher. It was there from California, owned by a dentist and his wife, an airline attendant. I could not help wondering what stories that aircraft could tell.

At the awards dinner, someone at the table asked if "so-and-so" was attending this year. The tone of the conversation became hushed, and several looked down at their fried chicken and mashed potato dinners on foam plates.

"No, he's not here."

One by one, comments circulated around the table.

"What's his marital situation?"

"Soon there won't be a marital situation."

"I could never see the match with his third wife."

"Boy is she smart--a really sharp lawyer."

"You know, everything is in her name: the house and all its contents."

"I knew all three of his wives; the first one was real nice."

In affairs of the heart and pecuniary matters, the pilot had struggled. At one point he had lived in a "shack" at an airport. But he had managed to keep his Waco. Years back it had gotten so tough he had put out a call for help to the Club. He was about to lose his airplane and would accept contributions from individuals. One member had tithed three thousand dollars.

After dinner we stepped out onto the ramp to admire a beautiful sunset. The sound of a radial engine rumbled as a pilot moved his precious machine to a hangar for the night. I thought of the man and his difficulties. Creve Coeur means "broken heart" in French.

KEEP 'EM FLYING

—⁂—

Airplanes need parts to stay in the air. A scattered army of skilled craftsmen emerges to meet the need for engines and airframe components.

THE TYPE CLUBS ARE THE HEART AND SOUL of the Waco community, but it takes hardware to keep these old planes in the air. A cottage industry has emerged to fill the need.

Waco '923 is powered by a seven-cylinder, 670-cubic-inch radial engine producing 225 horsepower at 1,800 rotations per minute. This Continental W670 engine was used in over a dozen other aircraft of the era and several light armored fighting vehicles during World War II.

Bob Hitchcock overhauled Waco '923's engine after the wreck. At his shop in Florida, he has this to say, "The atomic bomb saved my life. I had been drafted and put through advanced infantry training. We were on a troop ship, preparing to invade the Japanese homeland, when President Truman decided to go ahead and drop the bomb. It pleased the hell outa me and a lot of others." Bob stayed in the service four more years, trained as a military aircraft mechanic, and maintained P-38s and P-51s in the Aleutian Islands and elsewhere in Alaska. He kicked around for a while after the war, then obtained his civilian mechanic's license from East Coast Aero Tech in 1952. Initially he couldn't find a job in aviation, so he worked in a heavy machine shop overhauling big Caterpillar diesel engines.

He and a friend set up a small aircraft maintenance shop in Belfast, Maine, where he received FAA repair station status. The Feds would travel up from Portland every year to inspect the shop, and Bob saved all the rejected parts with their red tags to demonstrate how stringent he was in engine overhaul. Bob is a meticulous recordkeeper and collector of relevant information. He has a large collection of manufacturers' maintenance and overhaul manuals, some dating to World War II. His skills are such that the Owls Head Transportation Museum asked him to overhaul a rarity: a World War I Hispano-Suiza V8 engine. This required an excellent machine shop, as parts were obviously not available.

Bob figures he has overhauled over a hundred Continental W670 engines, at an average rate of three per year and a price of $20,000 to $22,000 for an outright sale, or

$16,000 to $17,000 for an overhaul/exchange. He's seen one engine run 1,400 hours before overhaul, but the core did not have much value. Maximum time between overhauls is usually 1,200 hours. The key to extended engine life is frequently checking the oil screen. If the engine starts "making metal," that is where the fragments will end up.

BUSINESS HAS SLOWED FOR BOB: "AT ONE TIME I WAS OVERHAULING FIVE ENGINES A YEAR, BUT NOW MOST ALL OF THIS IS SUPPORTED BY SOMEBODY'S HOBBY. THERE ARE A FEW SCENIC RIDE OPERATORS." ASKED IN 2012 IF HE HAS A SUCCESSOR FOR HIS BUSINESS, BOB LAMENTS, "NO, NO ONE HAS SHOWN ANY INTEREST IN IT."

Hydraulic lock is a bugaboo with radial engines, unlike flat (horizontally opposed) engines. Oil or fuel can leak past piston rings on cylinders near the bottom of the circle. When the engine is turned over, instead of the piston coming down on compressible air, it faces incompressible fluid. The forces on engine components are enormous, and something has to give, typically the connecting rod between the crankshaft and piston.

"THIS IS WHAT HAPPENS WHEN AN ARTICULATING CONNECTING ROD SAYS HELLO TO A CRANKSHAFT
COUNTERWEIGHT. THIS CAME FROM THE OWL'S HEAD TRANSPORTATION MUSEUM. ALL THEIR
VOLUNTEERS ARE FLAT ENGINE, NOT RADIAL ENGINE PILOTS. THIS ENGINE WAS STARTED TOO
LEAN, KICKED BACKWARD, SUCKED IN OIL, AND BENT THE ROD. SOME PILOTS DON'T REALIZE
THAT A LEAN MIXTURE START BURNS MUCH HOTTER AND FASTER THAN A RICH MIXTURE."

Bob takes care to balance his engines carefully using special equipment, weighing
individual rotating and reciprocating parts and adding weight to crankshaft counter-
weights as needed. He can only add weight to engine components, not remove any, lest
parts be weakened. Bob says, "I might have fifty or sixty serviceable pistons on the shelf,
if I find one that needs replacing, I can sort through and find within five grams of the
same weight. The crankshafts are the tough ones to balance; they need to be within half
a gram, and sometimes I've spent four or five hours in frustration trying to balance one.

Some days I would give up at the end of the day, remove all the weight I had added, and start over the next morning. All my engines get balanced and test run, and I can overhaul my own magnetos and carburetors." He set up his engine overhaul shop in Citra, Florida, in 1986, with a smaller shop near Deer Island, Maine.

Bob soloed a Stearman in the CPTP shortly before the program was cancelled. After the war he wanted to rebuild a UPF-7 and bought a basket case in eastern Massachusetts, paying $50 in cash plus a .22-caliber pistol. He has owned a series of airplanes and was actively flying his UPF-7 at age eighty-five. Bob Hitchcock and his wife both passed away in 2019.

THE M3 STUART LIGHT TANK SEEN IN ACTION AT GUADALCANAL IN 1942 (ABOVE), AND IN CUTAWAY (NEXT). IT USED THE CONTINENTAL RADIAL ENGINE.

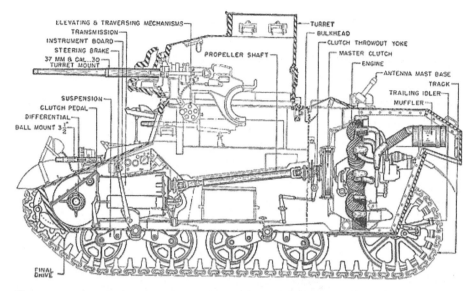

READERS WHO WOULD LIKE TO EXPERIENCE THE SIGHTS AND SOUNDS OF THIS ENGINE IN A WORLD WAR II ARMORED VEHICLE ARE URGED TO ATTEND PACIFIC COMBAT ZONE, A LIVING HISTORY LIVE-FIRE DEMONSTRATION HELD ON WEEKENDS AT THE NATIONAL MUSEUM OF THE PACIFIC WAR IN FREDERICKSBURG, TEXAS. IT IS AN EXCEPTIONAL MUSEUM.

THE CYLINDERS ON WACO '923'S ENGINE WERE DESTINED FOR A LIGHT TANK OR ARMORED CAR. WITHOUT A PROPELLER OR SLIPSTREAM TO COOL THE CYLINDERS, A POWERFUL FAN AND SHROUDS TO DUCT THE AIR WERE PLACED IN THE FRONT OF THE ENGINE. THE MOUNTING STUDS FOR THE SHROUD WERE CUT OFF WHEN THE CYLINDERS FOUND THEIR WAY TO AN AIRCRAFT.

The Waco came from the factory in 1940 with a metal propeller. Metal propellers are more efficient than wooden propellers, providing higher climb rates and cruising speeds. However, they are harder to come by and quite expensive. There is a limited supply of original propellers, and some have been damaged beyond repair. Supposedly, the wooden propeller is easier on the engine since the wood can absorb power pulses, and there is no question that it has better ramp appeal while the aircraft is on static display.

WACO '923'S PROPELLER AFTER TANGLING WITH THE BIRCH TREE ON CANNON MOUNTAIN.

THE SENSENICH COMPANY HAS BEEN MAKING WOODEN PROPELLERS SINCE 1932. EIGHT PIECES OF HIGH-GRADE BIRCH ARE LAMINATED, SHAPED, BALANCED, AND FINISHED. A PROPELLER COSTS ABOUT $4,000.

A responsible aircraft owner takes every precaution to avoid this scenario, but if a wooden propeller is left outside in the rain, it is to be left in the horizontal position. Otherwise water will settle in the lower end, and the prop will run out of balance. There are small holes in the metal leading edges to sling the water out.

Waco '923's battered wings were rebuilt by the Shues. Such is their craftsmanship and reputation that *AOPA Pilot* magazine published a full-length article about them in 2014:

> There's nothing about the two-story brick building in the small central Pennsylvania town of Emigsville to suggest that the two master craftsmen inside create some of the world's finest vintage biplanes.

For nearly 30 years, the father-and-son team of John and Scott Shue has quietly turned out Waco biplanes of exceptional quality using the same old-world techniques as the original builders in the 1930s.

FATHER AND SON STAND BEFORE WACO RESTORATIONS.

John restored his first Waco, a tattered World War II-era UPF–7 trainer, in the mid-1960s and then-5-year-old Scott assisted with menial tasks such as scrubbing the bare fuselage tubing with a wire brush. Since then, the two have re-created many flying works of art, including nine that have won top awards at prestigious competitions such as EAA AirVenture in Oshkosh...

The Shues have made a habit of buying surplus parts wherever and whenever they found them. "When I find Waco parts, I buy them," John says. "I think I've got at least one of just about everything the company ever made." The Shues used to sell surplus parts, but now some parts in their 50-year-old inventory are so rare, the parts are too valuable for their own use to let go...

The Shues have rented a hangar at the airport for more than a half-century, but they insist on doing restorations at their off-airport shop. They say it's more cost-effective for them to stay at a place that's already paid for, and with few distractions. They say moving to an airport would increase restoration costs, and have no desire to go anywhere else.

A local group of pilots and restorers comes by the shop once a week to share stories and go to a local diner for lunch. No one minds when Scott has classic rock on the radio, and he doesn't have to ask permission to bring his yellow Labrador retriever to the shop...

The father and son have seldom been apart more than two weeks since Scott was born, and their respect and affection for each other is obvious. "Scott's a far better woodworker than I ever was," John says. "He's an artist. He's so meticulous it's unbelievable.

Scott shrugs off the compliment. "He's just as meticulous as I am," Scott says of his dad. "All my work habits come from him."

"I love woodwork, and it's the part of every aircraft restoration that I enjoy most," says Scott, 54, whose Harley-Davidson T-shirt and faded jeans reveal a passion for motorcycles. "I know I could take shortcuts and use staples instead of nails in the wing ribs. But there's a challenge in doing things right—and I get a lot of satisfaction in knowing that everything on our airplanes is done as original—even if they're deep inside the airframe in places no one else can see."

Scott puts a final coat of varnish on a set of Waco wings he's about to complete, and the wood glistens in shafts of morning sunlight that shoot in through the shop's high windows. The wood spars are Sitka spruce from coastal Alaska, and the wing tips are mahogany plywood, just like the originals...

The Shues cover and paint their restorations using labor-intensive techniques that create lustrous colors and textures. It took 39 coats of butyrate dope, for example, to get the creamy, sky-blue finish they wanted on one of their current projects. The Shues' way takes more patience and skill than other methods—but they know their airplanes will stand up over time...

"Scott was a little kid when we restored our first Waco, but he was helpful all the way through," says John, 82, who later taught his son to fly in that airplane and watched him solo it on his sixteenth birthday—a snowy February morning in 1975. "He's been helping me ever since, and now he's surpassed me. Scott's a master woodworker and people all over the world come to him when they want wings."

The father and son have worked side by side so long, they can anticipate and deflect each other's barbs. When John teases his son for being "so damn finicky" about his work, Scott's pat response is a disarming smile."*

Replacement ailerons are in demand thanks to hangar rash, hail damage, ground loops, and complete restorations. By the 1980s, factory tooling was long gone, so Tom Flock reverse engineered the ailerons, throwing away three prototypes before he was happy. He filled a valuable niche and cranked out 850 ailerons over the years. Flock was later diagnosed with cancer and asked Tom Brown of Hartford, Wisconsin, to stand ready to take over the business.

A ROLLING DIE CONVERTS FLAT ALUMINUM SHEET TO CORRUGATED MATERIAL.

---

* Reprinted with the kind permission of the Aircraft Owners and Pilots Association.

AN ASSEMBLY FIXTURE ENSURES AN INTERCHANGEABLE PRODUCT. TOM REPORTS A LOWER
AILERON TAKES ABOUT TWELVE HOURS TO BUILD (NINE HOURS FOR AN UPPER).

As Tom Brown recounted in an interview with the author, "One day the phone
rang, and Tom said, 'You better get down here.' I drove over, and we spent a day and a
half making components—didn't finish a complete aileron but made the key parts. I
came home and right away made several ailerons so I wouldn't forget. Three weeks later
Tom Flock was gone. I've made about three hundred more ailerons."

A FINISHED AILERON GLEAMS ON TOM'S BEAUTIFULLY RESTORED UPF-7.

When Waco went out of business, the aircraft's type certificates and drawings became public domain. In 1983 the WACO Aircraft Corporation was founded in Battle Creek, Michigan, to bring the old bird back to life. Of all Waco's biplanes, the 1935 YMF was considered the most beautiful, and there were plenty of Jacobs engines available. Over three hundred engineering changes were made to improve the design and bring it to current standards. These are luxurious aircraft, many equipped for instrument flight with a glass cockpit and autopilot. More than 150 have been sold, and they are popular with scenic-ride air tour operators. The company does not support legacy Waco aircraft.

FLYING THE WACO

Improvements in modern aircraft design are evident to those learning to fly the Waco. Acquiring those skills is rewarded by the thrill of flying open cockpit in a classic machine from yesteryear.

—⚏—

"AFTER THE LAST WACO GRACEFULLY FLIES, THE SKY will become merely air."

The motto of the American WACO Club is not likely to be tested, as there will always be a Waco flying. Even after one has been wrecked, another is being lovingly restored… this in spite of the aircraft's flight characteristics. Compared to modern aircraft, the UPF-7 is a primitive and demanding machine. Most light aircraft have three wheels: a big one under each wing and a little one somewhere else. The Waco's bad habits derive from the little wheel being under the tail, not the nose. Known as "conventional" landing gear, this configuration was standard for planes of the 1920s and '30s.

All tailwheel aircraft have several things in common. On the ground, their noses are pointed in the air, which limits the pilot's view during taxi, takeoff, and landing. While taxiing from the hangar to the runway, the pilot is compelled to make S-turns, as a snake slithering along, since there is little forward visibility. An untold number of accidents have occurred when pilots taxied into another plane they did not see.

PILOT'S-EYE VIEW FROM THE WACO REAR COCKPIT, WITH A PERIPHERAL VIEW OF GROUND
AND NONE STRAIGHT AHEAD. SINCE THE PURPOSE OF THE WACO WAS TO TEACH BEGINNERS
TO FLY, THE STUDENT PILOT WAS PLACED IN THE FRONT COCKPIT, WITH BETTER VISIBILITY.
THE INSTRUCTOR, WITH MORE EXPERIENCE, GOT THE SECOND-CLASS SEAT IN BACK.

On takeoff roll, another tailwheel limitation becomes clear: the pilot can't see down the runway and has to use peripheral vision to keep the airplane lined up. The rudder is initially ineffective since there is little airflow and it is masked by the fuselage. The Waco has a tail wheel lock to add stability during takeoff and landing. Controllability gets better as air moves by the tail, the pilot pushes the stick forward to bring it up, and the plane assumes a flying attitude.

Cruise flight is like that of most other aircraft, except seeing and avoiding other planes is impeded by the pilot's view being blocked by the upper and lower wings. The pilot must keep his head on a swivel and make frequent turns to make sure the way is clear.

Landings are challenging since, unlike during takeoff, the pilot doesn't know exactly how high he is above the ground. Using peripheral vision to make a smooth landing requires practice, and each landing in the Waco is an experience. This is fun on nice days with light winds straight down the runway.

When the wind is strong and gusty *across* the runway, landing is another matter entirely. Airplanes by design are good weathervanes and tend to turn directly into the wind...leading the plane off the runway and into the puckerbrush. The pilot has to push the control stick toward the upwind side and press the downwind rudder pedal to keep the plane on the runway. These control movements must change constantly with gusty, unsteady winds, and they lose effectiveness as the aircraft slows. The goal is to get the tail on the ground so tailwheel steering and differential braking can assume directional control. It can be quite a ride.

The center of gravity of a tailwheel aircraft is behind the main wheels, and the tail of the aircraft will change places with the nose if the controls are mishandled. Even if the pilot maintains directional control, he cannot apply brakes too heavily lest the aircraft flip over end to end, leaving him hanging upside down with a bent propeller and broken tail.

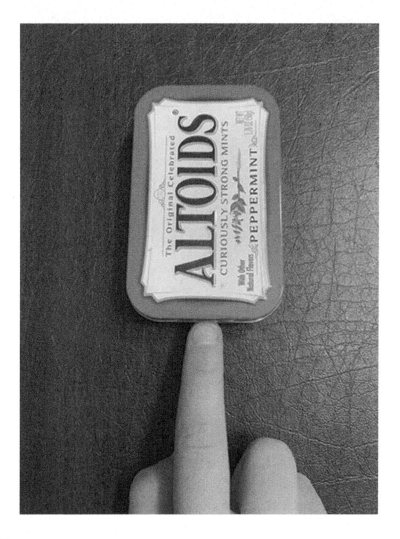

DEMONSTRATE THE CHALLENGE WITH A SMALL CANDY BOX, PUSHING IT ACROSS A SMOOTH TABLETOP WITH ONE FINGER. YOU CAN KEEP IT IN A STRAIGHT LINE BY WATCHING THE BOX AND MAKING SMALL ADJUSTMENTS, LEFT AND RIGHT.

IF YOU PUSH TOO QUICKLY OR OFF TO ONE SIDE, THE BOX SPINS AROUND AND
OFF THE END OF YOUR FINGER, AND YOU HAVE LOST CONTROL. THE CANDY BOX
ISN'T HURT, BUT A TAILWHEEL AIRCRAFT MOST LIKELY WILL BE.

The key objective in a crosswind landing is to minimize left or right movement across the runway during touchdown. With the center of gravity behind the main wheels, any drift when the wheels touch means the aircraft will swing around. If the drift is great, the swing exceeds the pilot's control authority, and the dreaded ground loop ensues. The plane may drag a wingtip, damage an aileron, break wing ribs and the spar, or collapse the landing gear—this sequence being set in motion because the pilot did not sense this translation across the runway or adequately correct for it.

These aircraft were not considered particularly difficult to fly in the 1930s because they were the standard of the times. The introduction of the nosewheel made aircraft easier to handle on the ground and has inadvertently produced generations of pilots who barely use their feet on the rudder pedals. Dedicated training and an endorsement to a pilot's license are required to operate a tailwheel aircraft.

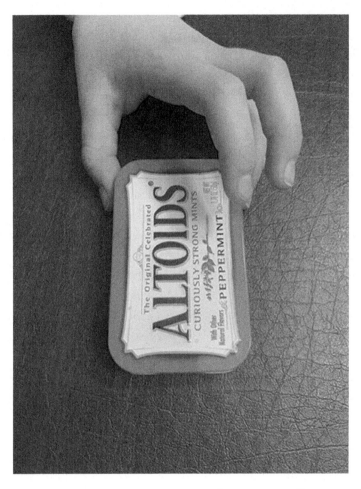

AIRPLANES WITH THE LITTLE WHEEL UP FRONT ARE CALLED "TRICYCLE GEAR" AIRCRAFT, PERHAPS BECAUSE THEY ARE SO MUCH EASIER TO FLY. THE CENTER OF GRAVITY IS IN FRONT OF THE MAIN WHEELS. PULL THE SAME CANDY BOX WITH TWO FINGERS INSTEAD OF PUSHING IT WITH ONE TO SEE HOW STABLE IT IS.

Cockpit visibility in nosewheel aircraft is great, and there is no tendency to ground loop or nose over—none of the nasty ground-handling habits. Crosswind takeoffs and landings are much easier. Tricycle gear aircraft fly on many windy days while tailwheel aircraft remain in the hangar. Students of aircraft design will note the transition from tailwheel to nosewheel aircraft during World War II. Too many aircraft were being torn up training pilots after the war, so the military switched to tricycle gear for both basic and advanced models

The Waco has large-diameter, low-pressure tires designed for grass airfields. They have a large footprint to resist sinking into the ground. However, these tires are a handicap when landing on a paved runway. The heavy tires require lots of energy to spin up on touchdown. The pilot feels this as a sudden grab and slight pitch forward. On landing in a crosswind, the upwind tire grabs first and tends to turn the plane even more into the wind, despite the pilot's efforts. Landing on grass is much easier since the tires slide over the surface and spin up more slowly.

Such are the pleasures of operating a tailwheel plane, but why would a pilot wish to fly such an aircraft? If a pilot chooses to fly an antique or bush-country plane, the choices in nosewheel aircraft are quite limited. The tailwheel does have one enduring advantage—operations on a rough, unimproved airstrip. The engine leans back, so propeller-tip ground clearance is greater. An aircraft's main landing gear is more robust by design than either a tail- or nosewheel. It supports most of the aircraft's weight and takes most of the punishment. With heavy braking on landing, the nosewheel tends to "wheelbarrow," or get buried in front. Many nosewheels have been damaged by landing on rough terrain or even a mishandled landing on pavement.

Heavy braking has the opposite effect in a tailwheel aircraft, with the robust main landing gear absorbing most of the energy. This is why many prefer these aircraft for operations on unimproved backwoods airports. Some of these planes are equipped with large, low-pressure "tundra tires" for very rough airstrips. Of course, excessive braking means the aircraft can flip forward onto its back, which will not happen with a nosewheel. Aviation is full of compromises.

One of the less enjoyable tasks associated with owning '923 was servicing the Waco's tailwheel. Ideally, you laid a piece of old carpet on the hangar floor and slithered under the horizontal stabilizer with a little air compressor. Engine oil runs back along the aircraft belly, making the bottom of the tail a nasty place. A solid rubber tailwheel has been developed for the Stearman and would be a nice addition to the Waco.

One of the most important preflight items is making sure the magnetos are off and pulling propeller blades through to check for hydraulic lock. A little oil is always left in the engine on shutdown. This makes for a swirling blue cloud of smoke and a sweet smell the next time the engine is started.

My best advice on flying the Waco, also applicable to other aircraft, came after we sold it. In researching this book, I came across "Waco Ground School with Captain Bud" in a club newsletter and talked to him by phone. Bud Fuchs spent 38 years with the airlines, retiring on the Boeing 767. He has nine hundred hours in the Douglas DC-3 and has owned a dozen airplanes, half of them tailwheel. He imparted the following advice:

Walt Kelly's Pogo said, "We have met the enemy and he is us." The only enemy a Waco has is rust and us!

Ailerons are the single most abused, and misunderstood, control on the aircraft, thanks to the introduction of the nosewheel. At low speed in a quartering crosswind, the tail is stalled; the angle of attack is too high. But the Waco's ailerons are mostly not stalled, and there are four of them with large surface area. On takeoff the ailerons should be turned hard on the stops into the known crosswind. The aileron on the downwind side will create more lift, thus more drag, pulling the plane in that direction. Known as "adverse yaw," this will effectively steer the airplane, opposing the weather vane tendency, engine torque, propeller factor, and runway slope. With increasing speed, the rudder comes alive and increases directional control.

The rule of thumb on the runway is always, always keep the ailerons proportionately opposite to the rudder. At landing approach speed, little aileron may be needed. However, as the flying machine slows, one foot will eventually find the firewall. Feeding in opposite aileron will keep her straight to taxiway turnoff speed. What we have lost with the introduction of the nosewheel is the forward slip to touchdown, and especially using adverse yaw as a primary directional control device on rollout, and the rudder gives up its authority by stalling out.

Captain Bud recommends an excellent exercise: unlocking the tail wheel and taxiing up and down a long runway, all the while keeping the aircraft straight using proportional and opposite aileron and rudder as wind conditions vary. He believes the lack of proper aileron use is aggravated in aircraft with control yokes versus joysticks—it may take a more exaggerated motion to reach the stop. He enumerates the control functions as One, Two, Three:

The elevator has only one job: controlling the pitch of aircraft, up and down.

The rudder has two jobs: directional control of the aircraft, left and right, and opposing adverse yaw.

The ailerons have three jobs: banking the aircraft in turns, banking to compensate for drift across the ground, and contributing adverse yaw.

I'm learning to fly
But I ain't got wings
Coming down is the hardest thing
I'm learning to fly
Around the clouds
But what goes up
Must come down
I'm learning to fly

—Tom Petty and the Heartbreakers

THE SNOWBIRD FLIES SOUTH

—w—

The eleventh owner of Waco '923 flew her in freezing weather to a new home in Mississippi. His dream of 'flying by the seat of your pants' came true.

IN NOVEMBER 2017 WE SOLD WACO '923 TO Tom Bullion. He relates his experience:

I learned to fly in Little Rock, Arkansas, soloing just before I went off to college. I had a stint in the Army, then went back to school and earned my Private license. I bought 1/6th of a Cessna 180 to sky dive out of. I learned to jump in the Army and loved it. I moved to Memphis, Tennessee, in 1973 to go to work for Federal Express, retiring after thirty years.

Fifty years of flying and I can see the sun setting on my flying experience. I wanted to listen to the wires and fly some aerobatics. I wanted to enjoy a wide landing gear which brought me to a UPF-7. I had been looking for one for over twelve years…all the airplanes had something that did not fit (usually money).

Tom got word that our Waco was for sale:

A quick call to John and my partner, Steve Brillard (FedEx Boeing 777 captain), and I flew up to inspect the airplane. Steve is an Airframe & Powerplant mechanic with Inspection Authorization and has flown UPF-7s since he was a youngster on Long Island towing gliders. Bill Midon and John Wood have taken excellent care of NC29923, upgrading the avionics to comply with the 2020 ADS-B standard. The aircraft is forest green with cream trim, with 350 hours on both the 25-year-old restoration by Chris Cunningham and on the engine. She is in nice shape and looks pretty good even after 25 years.

We bought the airplane and started flying her home from New Bedford, Massachusetts, with a temperature on the ground of 19 degrees Fahrenheit. We stopped at Danbury, Connecticut to check fuel and oil consumption and weather before going over the mountains. The weather was terrible, and we stayed two days waiting for the weather to clear. We went to a sporting goods store and bought every warm piece of clothing we could afford.

We decided to fly over the Pocono Mountains on the 1930's CAM-1 airmail route. We had *monster* headwinds and flew as close to the ground as we could at 5,400 feet with an outside air temperature of 2 degrees. Those mail pilots of old were tough hombres, I tell ya! We departed Danbury and after 2 hours and 15 minutes landed in Reedsville, Pennsylvania. I was so cold I could not feel the rudder pedals. Fueling the UPF-7 without a ladder, frozen to the bone, and being over 70 years old is a challenge. Still fighting a headwind we're off to Parkersburg, West Virginia to remain overnight and were happy to put NC29923 in a heated hangar. We stayed across the Ohio River in a hotel built in 1918 (I had an original bed) and our bar tab was more than the room.

Late the next morning we were off to Charleston, West Virginia, then Georgetown, Kentucky. Still bucking a headwind (I hope the plane loses this trait) we stopped at Selmer, Tennessee and then to our home base of Olive Branch, Mississippi. Total flying time was just over 16 hours, and worth every minute of it. She flies hands off which is helpful when changing radio frequencies, warming hands and stamping feet.[1]

Tom Bullion at Waco '923's new home in Mississippi.

FINAL MISSION

—ᴡ—

Nostalgia alone may be all that is needed to keep Waco '923 flying toward its 100th birthday and beyond. It requires airmanship skills that have atrophied in the era of the digital airplane.

I THINK OF THE WACO'S LIFE IN THREE phases—youth, middle age, and retirement. Early on, the aircraft served as an advanced teaching aid. CPTP students soloed and learned the basics in a Piper Cub or equivalent, and next they were exposed to aerobatics in the Waco. For pilots who went on to fly transports or bombers, this was a matter of checking the box. These aviators would most likely never use the skills they learned doing spins, loops, and rolls. Fighter pilots, on the other hand, might employ some of these maneuvers on each mission.

In middle age the Waco was well suited for the tough, messy work of crop dusting. It was a great load hauler that was cheap to purchase and easy to work on, and spare parts were plentiful. Who knows how much wheat or how many apples were harvested in central Washington thanks to Waco '923?

In old age the Waco came to be respected as a relic from a bygone age in aviation. I volunteered in bringing the plane to several air shows for static display. As families with children approached, I would hear the oohs and aahs. "Wow, a wooden propeller and a round engine!" I felt as though I had a live pterodactyl beside me on a leash. I've hoisted countless kids up into the rear cockpit and watched them study the controls. I wonder how many may have gone on to aviate.

"Say souls on board" is a sobering request from an air traffic controller when an aircraft may be in trouble. The phrase is not taught in air traffic controller training, but everyone understands the urgency. It conveys a request for the number of people on board, whether passengers or crew.

According to a controller's newsletter, "The concept of counting souls on board a vessel dates back at least to the first century, with nautical references in the Bible. But contrary to what English speakers might think today when they hear the word 'soul,' the Greek word for it didn't have a spiritual meaning."[1]

I have thought of the spiritual connotation of the phrase more than once while flying Waco '923. If this aircraft has been flying for almost eighty years, how many souls

195

could be along with me today? Even if just one new person flew or rode in the plane every week, the total would be over four thousand.

Those who served in World War II immediately come to mind. I talked to several old-timers for whom the long-forgotten airplane held a special place. After aerobatic training in the Waco, some went on to fly as pilots, others flew in different roles, and others still were screened out of aviation and served elsewhere. Unfortunately, I did not hear from those who did not come home.

Bill and I each flew the Waco about two hundred hours over twelve years. We did not "own" this airplane; we were stewards. We were fiduciaries, responsible for something that did not belong to us. Fly on, Waco '923, toward the hundred-year mark of 2040.

FLY ON, WACO '923, TOWARD THE HUNDRED YEAR MARK OF 2040.*

---

* No, this photo was not the result of a formation flight. The author built a camera mount and attached it to an outer strut between the wings. A remote camera release is barely visible in his right hand at the bottom of the windscreen.

Bill will wrap it up:

I was able to share the Waco experience with my children, my children's friends, wife, numerous friends, and some outstanding instructors. Sharing my aviation passion and providing a "once-in-a-lifetime" open-cockpit flying experience for many was an incredible blessing. I am filled with gratitude for Chris Cunningham's passion and superb craftsmanship in bringing NC29923 back to life. It deserved nothing less. Chris and his mom, Dot, will always bring back a flood of fond memories.

I enjoy sharing with other pilots that in 2016, our venerable Waco was the oldest aircraft on the airport but among the first to be ADS-B compliant. Waco '923 was ahead of its time for once. That John and I were stewards twice as long as any previous owner, and did not wreck the airplane, was a blessing. She had been reduced to a basket case by too many wrecks. The engine, dating to 1943, never quit on us—this was a gift. On both counts I am reminded sometimes it is better to be lucky than good! Do I miss our Waco? Only on every blue-sky, sunny day...even in the dead of winter. But what a blessing to have known her for those twelve memorable years!

BIPLANING IS...
To see a rainbow in the round
To land upon a cloud
The breath of freedom brushing brow
To hear the vibrant sound

Of wires whistlin' in the wind
Warm sunshine on my back
To glide beside the highest ridge
And view the glacier pack

To porpoise freely way up there
Behind round engine smells
To never land, to yell all clear
And peel off in chandelles
—Lorraine Duncan, friend of Dorothy Fowler

ACKNOWLEDGMENTS

—m—

RESEARCH FOR THIS BOOK WAS TRIGGERED BY MY request for aircraft airworthiness and ownership records from the FAA. To my surprise they ran several hundred pages and went back to delivery in 1940. Some owners had uncommon surnames, which were easy to search online. I would like to acknowledge the people who received my phone call or letter that began, "I found your name on the internet and wonder if you are related to so-and-so, who was a pilot." Luckily I began the interviews in 2005, when several World War II veterans were still with us. Many were impressed that the Waco is still flying and were generous with their time, recollections, and photographs. Frequently one contact led to another: "You should really talk to..." Many thanks to the following:

Judith Adkins, Max Alumbaugh, Mel Alumbaugh, Wylie Apte Jr., Richard Baxter, Roger Bertsch, Steve Brillard, Randall Brink, Dennis Buehn, Tom Brown, Tom Bullion, Rob Burbank, Dorothy Buroker, Kelly Buroker, Linda Buroker-Melhoff, Mary Chapman, Judith Cirone, Chris Cunningham, Dot Cunningham, Glenn Davison, Dick Deans, John Dickson, Deborah DiPhilippo, Roger Durham, Sandy Emerson, Eldon Flahaut, Betty Fowler, Dorothy Fowler, Jack Fowler, David Frawley, Bud Fuchs, Wayne Gaffney, Barry George, George Gewehr, Roger Guilmette, Herb Hart, Bob Hitchcock, Nancy Hitchcock, Edward Johnson, Bob Kennington, Gordon Kennington, Bernard and Ira Laurie, Gary Libra, Forrest Lovley, Art Lucas, Mary Lyons, Alana MacDonald, Reinhold May, Roger Marcoux, Patricia Martell, McAllister Museum of Aviation, Bruce McKay, Robert Moore, Marilynn Moses, Chuck Naasz, Clara Nugent, Patrick O'Grady, Okanogan Community Library, Okanogan County Historical Society, Verne Partlow, Chris Peatridge, Stan Parker, Eric Paul, Scott Shue, Sally Simundson, Charles Sprague, Jay Stout, Steve Stratford, Lee Swain, Jessica Sylvannus, Betty Thompson, Keith Thompson, Renee Townsley, Anna Mae Trohimovich, Barbara Trohimovich, Josh Tuttle, Michael Twitchell, Howard Verbeck, June and James Walter, Brick Wellman, Tanner Wilson, and Mary Kay Wood.

Special thanks to Bill Midon, who was first an airplane partner and then became a good friend. Plus, his checks always clear at the bank which is important in joint aircraft ownership.

Thanks to Lydia, Byron, Jenny, and the rest of the team with Elite Authors.

Tom Widmer is best writer I knew on the job; he is a real wordsmith. I am grateful he took an interest in the book and made many useful suggestions.

ABOUT THE AUTHOR

—ɯ—

JOHN WOOD GRADUATED FROM LOUISIANA TECH UNIVERSITY AND the Massachusetts Institute of Technology. He studied engineering, retired as a public company CEO, and now serves as a corporate board member. Wood was company spokesman with high-profile exposure in print, television, and radio during investigations of the Pan Am 103 and TWA 800 crashes. On two occasions, he testified before the US Congress about improved airport security.

Rated as an airline transport pilot and certified flight instructor, Wood has logged seven thousand flight hours and has experience piloting over one hundred aircraft makes and models, including jets, turboprops, seaplanes, helicopters, gliders and bal-loons. Wood is a veteran public speaker and lives with his wife in Concord, Massachusetts. He has studied and adheres to the first principles of aviation:

1. Never get higher off the ground than you care to fall.

2. Never miss a chance to take a leak.

3. Don't land until you get to the airport—unless you are flying a helicopter.

NOTES

—⁓—

The Early Days

[1] Dominick A Pisano, *To Fill the Skies with Pilots* (Washington, Smithsonian Institution Press, Washington, 2001).

[2] Smithsonian National Air and Space Museum, Wall of Honor Location: Foil: 23 Panel: 3 Column: 1 Line: 21.

[3] Gladys Buroker with Fran Bahr, *Wind in My Face* (Coeur d'Alene, Action Printers, 1997).

[4] "City's airport started at fairgrounds," *The Coeur d'Alene Press*, March 17, 1997.

[5] Brigadier General Patrick O'Grady, Distinguished Military and Airline Pilot, *OX5 News*, Volume 39, Number 5, June 1997.

Freight Dog and the Mountain

[1] Linda Cameron, Civilian Conservation Corps in Minnesota, 1933–1942, *MNOPEDIA* http://www.mnopedia.org/civilian-conservation-corps-minnesota-1933-1942.

[2] "S/SGT Jack E. Seese, Radio Operator", OZ at War, https://www.ozatwar.com/people/jackseese.htm.

[3] Herb Hart and Gary Libra, in discussion and correspondence with the author.

[4] Rudy Libra, "Read Me the Roadmap," *Skyways*, October 1950.

[5] Wikipedia see Flying Tiger Line, https://en.wikipedia.org/wiki/Flying_Tiger_Line.

[6] Wikipedia see Airline Deregulation, https://en.wikipedia.org/wiki/Airline_deregulation

[7] Air Safety Network, see N6920C, September 9, 1958, https://aviation-safety.net/database/record.php?id=19580909-0.

[8] "Eight Americans Killed in Air Crash in Japan," *The Minneapolis Star*, September 9, 1958.

[9] Air Safety Network, see 42-72704, April 21, 1950, https://aviation-safety.net/database/record.php?id=19500421-0.

[10] "Rites Here for Flying Tiger Pilot," *Pasadena Independent*, September 24, 1958.

[11] George Gewehr, Historian, Flying Tiger Line Pilots Association, in correspondence with the author.

Death and Taxes

[1] Wikipedia, see Curtiss-Wright AT-9, https://en.wikipedia.org/wiki/Curtiss-Wright_AT-9

[2] Wikipedia, see North American B-25, https://en.wikipedia.org/wiki/North_American_B-25_Mitchell

[3] 345th Bomb Group, http://www.345thbombgroup.org/index.php

[4] Lawrence J. Hickey, *Warpath Across the Pacific*, (Boulder, International Historical Research Associates, 2008).

[5] Anna and Barbara Trohimovich, in correspondence with the author.

[6] People/Places, Ocean Breeze, J. M. Weatherwax High School, Aberdeen, WA, October 16, 1987.

[7] Stanley J. Trohimovich, "'Everything was a target' was a standing order," *The Daily World*, Aberdeen, WA, September 19, 1995).

[8] Trohimovich v. Commissioner of Internal Revenue, United States Tax Court, August 10, 1981, https://casetext.com/case/trohimovich-v-commissioner-of-internal-revenue

[9] "Longtime government watchdog Trohimovich dies," *The Daily World*, Aberdeen, WA, April 27, 2011.

[10] Wikipedia see Tax protester constitutional arguments, http://en.wikipedia.org/wiki/Tax_protester_constitutional_arguments.

The Great Lies

[1] Mabry I. Anderson, "The Move Westward," *Ag Aircraft Update*, (July 2017): B-4.

Snakes and Fire

[1] Max Alumbaugh, in discussion and correspondence with the author.

[2] "Two Lose Lives in Plane Crash," *Spokane Daily Chronicle*, October 17, 1955.

[3] Alumbaugh v. Underwriting Members of Lloyd's, Supreme Court of Washington, November 21, 1957.

[4] "Spray Pilot Strikes Power Line; Injured Seriously," *Okanogan Independent*, September 26, 1957.

[5] "Airline Sought by Alumbaugh," *Omak Chronicle*, April 26, 1962.

[6] "Charter Plane Gutted by Flames Last Friday," *Omak Chronicle*, February 28, 1963.

[7] "14-year-old boy killed in plane crash," *The Bulletin*, Sept 17, 1962.

[8] "Crash Claims Life of Pilot," *Okanogan Independent*, May 16, 1963; "Pilot's Funeral Held Tuesday," *Omak Chronicle*, May 16, 1963;

The Tooth Carpenter

[1] Obituary in *Spokesman-Review,* July 29, 2009.

[2] "Want an Airplane? It's Simple—Do It Yourself," *Spokane Valley Herald*, July 16, 1964.

[3] Jack and Dorothy Fowler, in discussion and correspondence with the author.

[4] "Sculptor, aviator created St. Ann's bronze doors," *Great Falls Tribune*, March 8, 2015.

[5] Dr. Jack Fowler, as told to Ross Woodward*: Looking back on Schweitzer,* (Spokane, Marshall Publishing Company, 1991).

Sunset Strip

[1] Judy Cirone, in discussion with author.

East to New England

[1] Wylie Apte, Jr., Obituary, *The Conway Daily Sun*, March 8, 2012.

[2] Wylie Apte, Jr., in correspondence with the author.

[3] Gordon Kennington and son Bob, in discussion with the author.

[4] White Mountain Airport (CWN), North Conway, NH*: Abandoned & Little-Known Airfields,* http://www.airfields-freeman.com,

I'm Never Going to Die in an Airplane

[1] Eric Paul, in discussion with the author, 2012.

[2] "Strange birds hooked on the exhilarating sport of flying," *The Irregular,* North Conway, NH, July 13, 1988.

I'll Never Forget What's-Her-Name

[1] "Lucky Ass Plane Crash Segment," *Real TV* video clip, February 18, 1997 episode.

My Grandfather's Ax

[1] Wikipedia, see Ship of Theseus, https://en.wikipedia.org/wiki/Ship_of_Theseus

Ground Loop!

[1] Mattapoisett Police Department Report, Narrative for Lieutenant Detective Paul Silveira, 2005.

[2] Mattapoisett Police Department Report, Narrative for Patrolman Craig S. Leblanc, 2005.

[3] Rob Margetta, "Ex-officer charged with forging checks," SouthCoastToday, January 14, 2011, https://www.southcoasttoday.com/article/20051224/news/312249996

[4] Rob Margetta, "Chief: Murder investigation unlikely in death of famed aviator Frawley, January 14, 2001, https://www.southcoasttoday.com/article/20051230/News/312309999

[5] Mary Lyons, Mattapoisett Police Chief, in correspondence with the author, 2019.

[6] Massachusetts Board of Bar Overseers, Disciplinary Decisions, In the Matter of Robert G. Moore, Public Reprimand No. 2009-07.

[7] Massachusetts Board of Bar Overseers, Disciplinary Decisions, In the Matter of Robert G. Moore, No. BD-2013-013.

[8] "Police say man stole from pilot who died in fall," *The Boston Globe,* December 24, 2005.

Broken Heart

[1] Waco CG-4A Hadrian, National Museum of the US Air Force, https://www.nationalmuseum.af.mil/Visit/Museum-Exhibits/Fact-Sheets/Display/Article/196272/waco-cg-4a-hadrian/

[2] David Hirschman, "Craftsmanship: Where Wacos Take Wing," *AOPA Pilot,* April 5, 2014.

[3] The National Waco Club, https://www.nationalwacoclub.com

[4] The American WACO Club, http://www.americanwacoclub.com

The Snowbird Flies South

[1] Tom Bullion Finds His UPF-7, *Waco WORLD NEWS,* Vol 1 #126, Second Issue 2018.

Epilogue

[1] "The Mystery of 'Souls on Board,'" *NATCA Insider,* November 4, 2016.

BOOKS AND MONOGRAPHS

—ᴍ—

American Airman 1, no.6 (February 1958.)

Anon, *The Life and Death of an Airman in the AAF, 1942-45,* http://squiz63.tripod.com/article.htm

Atwood, Bert L., *My Father Was a Crop Duster,* Kelseyville: AAAA Publishing, 2007

Balmer, Joe and Davis, Ken, *There Goes a Waco,* Troy: Little Otter Productions, 1991.

Brandly, Raymond H., *Taperwing Wacos,* 1984.

Brandly, Raymond H., *The Authentic History of Waco Airplanes,* 1988.

Brandly, Raymond H., *Waco Aircraft Production, 123-1942,* 1978.

Brandly, Raymond H., *Waco Airplanes, The Famous "F" Series,* 1982.

Brandly, Raymond H., *Waco Airplanes, The Versatile Cabin Series,* 1981.

Buroker, Gladys, *Wind in My Face,* Coeur d'Alene: Action Printers, 1997.

Craft, Stephen G., *Embry-Riddle at War,* University Press of Florida, 2009.

Emerson, Tom, *Hangar Flying, with Float Country Bush Pilot Stories,* Coeur d'Alene: 1988.

Emerson, Tom, *Seaplanes from Coeur d'Alene,* 1973.

Fowler, Dr. Jack, Woodward, Ross, *Looking Back on Schweitzer: The Story of Schweitzer Mountain Resort,* Spokane: Marshall Publishing, 1991.

Goodall, Geoff, Aviation History Website, https://www.goodall.com.au.

Hickey, Lawrence J., *Warpath Across the Pacific*, Boulder: International Historical Research Associates, 2008.

Kidder, Tracy & Todd, Richard, *Good Prose, The Art of Nonfiction*, Random House, 2013.

King, Stephen, *On Writing, A Memoir of the Craft*, Scribner, 2000.

Kobernuss, Fred O., *Waco, Symbol of Courage & Excellence*, Volume 2, Aviation Heritage Library Series, Mystic Bay Publishers, 1999.

Matt, Paul R. *Historical Aviation Album, All American Series*, Volume 8, Waco UPF-7 by Peter M. Bowers, 1970.

Pace, Robert E., *J. M. Perry, The Man & The School*, Yakima: Perry Technical Institute, 2000.

Pierce, Marilyn R., *Earning Their Wings: Accidents and Fatalities in the United States Army Air Forces During Flight Training in World War Two*, PhD Dissertation, Kansas State University, 2013.

Pisano, Dominick A., *To Fill the Sky with Pilots, The Civilian Pilot Training Program 1939-1946*, Chicago: University of Chicago Press, 1993.

Simpson, Rod & Trask, Charles, *WACO*, Stroud: Tempus Publishing Limited, 2000.

Stout, Jay A., *Air Apaches*, Stackpole Books, 2019.

BIRTH CERTIFICATE

Sales Order No. 242C

Serial No. 5420

AIRPLANE EQUIPMENT AND HISTORY RECORD

ENGINE MAKE & MODEL Continental W670-6A SERIAL NO. 5311 LICENSE NO. N29923 MODEL UPF-7

EQUIPMENT	MFGR.	Model	MODEL	Serial	Serial
Carburetor	Stromberg	NA-R6		5530948	
Magneto—Left	Scintilla	MN-7D		2033	
Magneto—Right	"	"		2018	
Starter (Elec-Electric)	Eclipse	E-80		279	
Prop. (Metel-Wood)	Curtiss Reed 55501 (102-63) /9150				
Radio	no				
Shock Struts	FRONT			REAR	
Tachometer	706 (2010-1A1-A1) Pioneer 2000-1A-A1			2640	
Altimeter	4112	Kollsman 126-011		4062	
Compass	2700	"	132-B	2632	
Airspeed	13364	Pioneer 1402-2D-C2		13307	
Turn Indicator					
Climb Indicator					
Clock	9359	Elgin(Pioneer)	3310-2-A	8924	
Door Lock (baggage)	Sesame				
Upholstering	Brown fabricoid #461				
Wheel Pants	no				
Wheels & Brakes	Hayes	7:50 x 10			
Tires	Goodyear	8:50 x 10			
Tail Wheel	Hayes	10" smooth contour			

PAINT SPECIFICATIONS (Indicate Trade Name of Colors)

MFGR.   FUSELAGE   WINGS   COWL   FIN. & RUD.   STAB. & FLIP.

Color   Fuselage and fin Army-Navy blue

Detail of Striping Wings, stabilizer and elevators Army-Navy yellow; all struts Army-Navy blue - license number in intense black

Record below all extra equipment such as streamline fairing, special cowling and wings. Also all changes of any nature from standard design.

Front and Rear Cockpits -

Kollsman oil pressure gauge - 143E-02

Kollsman oil temperature gauge - 131E-02

Booster Coil - #17

LEFT WHEEL   RIGHT WHEEL   TAIL WHEEL   TOTAL

Weight

Date Completed   10-1-40

Distributor _____ CAA

Dealer and Date Transferred _____

Owner and Date Transferred 10-10-40   9-24-42

Buroker Hicks Flying Service

~~Spokane, Washington~~ Coeur D'Alene, Idaho ~~6-12-1-45~~

Central Aircraft,

Box 1364 Uni. Apt., 3-18-46

Yakima, Washington.

RECORD OF OWNERSHIP

Date Delivered New 10-10-40

5420

Record below all free factory adjustments and the amount thereof at regular Distributors cost (use red ink). Also make note of all crack ups or major repairs.

Shpd. Buroker Hicks one complete set improved type strut point fittings Nos. 22933,22935,22932,22941 on S.P.R. #17696 of 1/11/41 (no charge)spars inspected and reinforced per general letter No. 686 and check sketch returned 5/12/41. Old type strut point fittings returned as per receivi record #35480 dated 5/28/41.

Shpd. Buroker Hicks one set longeron reinforcements #23590 per service bulletin #100. See S.P.R. #15566 dated 2/25/42 (no charge)

Coupon indicating SK613 complied with ret'd	3-24-41	
" SK614	3-24-41	
" SK617	11-20-41	
" SK626	12-20-40	
" SK627	12-10-40	
" SK633	1-19-41	
" SK642	3-24-41	
" SK643	3-24-41	
" SK649	5-3-41	
" SK668	5-3-41	
" SK671	4-2-41	
" SK683	6-11-41	
" SK689	5-29-41	
" SK694	5-3-41	
" SK 710	7-22-41	
" SK911	7-22-41	
" SK712	7-22-41	
" SK737	8-8-41	
" SK23046	11-20-40	
showing installation	3-24-41 returned	Drawing 22931
"	3-24-41	Drawing 22940
"	3-24-41	Drawing 22942
"	3-24-41	Drawing 22943

AIRPLANE WEIGHT RECORD
THE WACO AIRCRAFT CO.
TROY, OHIO.

MODEL UP 1 — SALES ORDER No. 2 1 ?
DATE WEIGHED 4-30-40 — DofC. LICENSE No. 29123 — SERIAL No. 5426

ENGINE.- MAKE _Cont_ — SERIAL No. 531
MODEL R-670-6A — H.P. 220 — WACO STD. WT.

EQUIPMENT NOT STANDARD.	MANUFACTURES NAME Description, Size, Etc.	ACTUAL WEIGHT	WEIGHT DIFFERENCE FROM STANDARD	
			PLUS	MINUS
PROPELLOR	Curtiss Reed 102 x 63			
SHIELDING				
EXTERNAL FINISH				
UPHOLSTERY				
WHEEL PANTS				
LANDING LIGHTS				
RADIO RECEIVER				
RADIO TRANSMITTER				
FLARES				
FUEL SYSTEM				
OIL SYSTEM				
TIRES	8.50 x 10			
TUBES				
BANK-TURN INDICATOR				
RATE OF CLIMB INDICATOR				
THERMOCOUPLE				
CLOCK				
MANI. PRESSURE GAGE				
DIRECTIONAL GYRO				
ARTIFICIAL HORIZON				
SHOCK PROOF INSTR. PANEL				
PARACHUTE CHAIRS				
DUAL CONTROL COLUMN				
STARTER				
GENERATOR				
SENSITIVE ALTIMETER				
AMBULANCE				
SKIIS				
METAL COCKPIT COVER				
COUPE TOP				
NET TOTAL.				
NET LOSS OR GAIN.				

DIFFERENCE FROM STD. WEIGHT — PLUS _____ LBS.
MINUS _____ LBS.

AIRPLANE AS WEIGHED INCLUDING EQUIPMENT NOT STANDARD _____ LBS.

1819 less 14 oil
120

USEFUL LOAD

		CON.PTY	CREW PASS. NO. LBS.	MAIN LBS.	AUX. GAL. LBS.	RES. GAL. LBS.	OIL GAL. LBS.	MISC DISPOS LBS.	BAGGAGE LBS.	TOTAL LBS.
	FUEL									
PAY LOAD										
		1								
		2								
		3								
		4								

SUMMARY

ALLOWABLE GROSS WEIGHT	
USEFUL LOAD	−
TOTAL	
ENGINE DIFFERENCE	±
TOTAL	
EQUIPMENT NOT STD.	±
EMPTY WT. AS STD. AIRPLANE	1587
ORIGINAL STD. WEIGHT	250
DIFFERENCE IN WEIGHT	± 1637

REMARKS:-
C.g. in forward of
L.W.L.E. 11.92"

PEREGRINATIONS

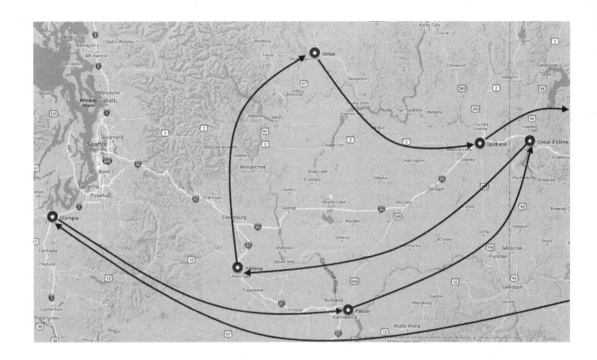

Home Bases for Waco UPF-7 NC29923

1940   Delivered from Waco factory in Troy, OH, to Civilian Pilot Training Program in Olympia, WA.

1942   Moved with the flight school to Pasco, WA, after civil flight along the coast was banned following the bombing of Pearl Harbor.

1942   Moved again with the flight school moved to Coeur d'Alene, ID, after US Navy took over Pasco airport.

1943   Sold back to the US government after Civilian Pilot Training Program ended.

1944   Sold to two private individuals in Yakima, WA.

1945   Purchased by Central Aircraft of Yakima, WA, and converted to a crop duster.

1955   Bought by Verne Alumbaugh, a crop duster based in Omak, WA.

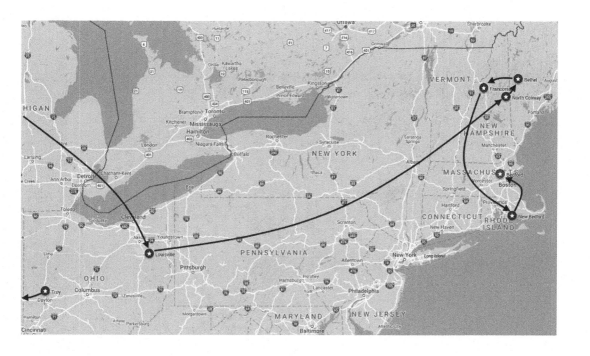

1961   Wreckage sold to Dr. Jack Fowler, a dentist in Spokane, WA. Rebuilt, replacing chemical hopper with front cockpit.

1974   Sold to Michael Cirone of Louisville, OH.

1975   Sold to Wylie Apte Jr. for his scenic air tour operation in North Conway, NH.

1982   Sold to Louis Paul for his scenic air tour operation in Gorham, NH.

1989   Sold to Stan Parker for his scenic air tour operation in Franconia, NH.

1993   Wreckage sold to David Frawley in New Bedford, MA.

2004   Sold to Bill Midon and John Wood in Bedford, MA.

2017   Sold to Tom Bullion in Olive Springs, MS.

GLOSSARY

—⚭—

ADS-B—automatic dependent surveillance-broadcast

CAA—Civil Aeronautics Administration

CAM-1—Contact Air Mail, Route 1

CCC— Civilian Conservation Corp

CPTP—Civilian Pilot Training Program

FAA—Federal Aviation Administration

Gosport—An acoustic speaking tube allowing the flight instructor to communicate with the student. Named for the British town where it was invented during World War I.

Localizer—the horizontal component of the Instrument Landing System that provides left/right guidance

Scud—low cloud overcast

TLA—three letter acronym

VHF—very high frequency

WTS—War Training Service

PHOTO CREDITS

—◊—

To see the author's 360-degree panoramas of Waco '923 visit the National Waco Club website, Waco Panorama:

https://www.nationalwacoclub.com/waco-aircraft/waco-panorama/

INDEX

DC-10, 79
DC-3, 30ff, 99, 126, 128ff, 151, 188
DC-9, 79, 100f
de Haviland Tiger Moth, 157
Demoulas, Louie, 100
DePhilippo, Deborah, 95f
Duncan, Lorraine, 197
Dunham, Roger, 91f

FBI, 163f
FDR, 1
Federal Express, 31, 191
Flock, Tom, 180f
Flying Tiger Line, 30ff
Ford Tri-Motor, 79
Fowler, Dorothy, 68ff
Fowler, Jack, 63ff
Frawley, Dave, 115ff, 122, 125ff, 151
Fuchs, Bud, 188f

Gallagher, Diana, 151ff
Gilead Bridge, 90
Great Lakes biplane, 63
Grumman Albatross, 133ff
Grumman Mallard, 79
Grumman Wildcat, 151
Guilmette, Roger, 90f

HH-43B, 60
HS-125, 128
Hampton Airfield, 143ff
Hart, Herb, 22ff
Hiroshima, 41
Historic Aircraft Restoration Museum, 166
Hitchcock, Bob, 169ff
Hughes, John, 47

Ie Shima, 41

J-3, 69, 99
J-5, 9

KC-97, 77
Katama Airpark, 142
Kennington, Gordon, 79
Key West, 93
Koresh, David, xi

L-1049H, 32ff
L-19, 93, 95, 102, 107
Lermer, Walt, 102
Libra, Gary, 34f
Libra, Rudy, 17ff
Lindbergh, Anne Morrow, 103
Lockheed 10, 126
Lovley, Forrest, 164ff
Lyons, Mary, 139

M3 Stuart Light Tank, 172f
MacDonald, Alana, 93
McArthur, Douglas, 21f
Marijuana, 87
Marquart Charger, 73
Meyers, William, 23
Midon, Bill, 141ff, 151, 191
Moore, Robert, 138ff

Nagasaki, 43
National Museum of the Pacific War, 173
National Waco Club, 163ff
New Bedford, 115ff, 125ff, 141, 151, 192
New Deal, 1
New England Escadrille, 128ff
Nugent, Jenny, 156

O'Grady, Patrick, 9ff
Omega BS-12, 127

Made in United States
North Haven, CT
15 January 2022

14828151R00128